Single
Servings

Single Servings

90 Devotions to Feed Your Soul

LEE WARREN

Revell
Grand Rapids, Michigan

Published by Fleming H. Revell
a division of Baker Publishing Group
P.O. Box 6287, Grand Rapids, MI 49516-6287

Printed in the United States of America

Library of Congress Cataloging-in-Publication Data
Warren, Lee, 1966–
    Single servings : 90 devotions to feed your soul / Lee Warren.
        p.   cm.
    Includes bibliographical references.
    ISBN 0-8007-5947-8
    1. Single people—prayer-books and devotions—English. I. Title.
BV4596.S5W37 2005
242′.64—dc22   2004027864

To Mom, for believing in me.
To Dad, for listening to me.
To Phil Kayser, for preparing me.
To Joy, for believing in my writing before I did.
To Vicki, for helping me clarify my message.
To my friends, for cheering me on.

Contents

Part 1

Community

Have you ever experienced the loneliness of a solitary Saturday night? Anything you do—from renting a movie to reading a good book—seems to magnify your feelings. Nobody is there to laugh with you during the comical parts of the movie. Nobody is there to listen to you read a passage from a book that moved you.

We all desire to connect with other people—to be loved, to share in the lives of others, and to have others share in our lives. God made us relational beings. To function properly, we need to be in right relationship not only with him but also with each other.

The problem is, our security-conscious, privacy-guarded, fast-paced society doesn't allow us to expand our community easily. We often don't know our next-door neighbor's name, let alone the rest of the people who live in our neighborhood. We've isolated ourselves by design.

In our seclusion, pangs of loneliness shoot through our souls, demanding that we search for someone who cares about us. Those pangs can hurt, but they are not inherently bad. They tell us that we need community—both with God and with other humans. The pangs remind us that we've spent too much time by ourselves.

For singles, the danger is thinking that the only way to get past this sense of loneliness is to find a potential spouse. However, the Bible points us to other resources: to family, friends, and the body of Christ—community.

In her book *Feast of Life*, Jo Kadlecek defines community: "Community . . . is a coming together, a joining with other flesh and blood that all humans in all cultures in all times of history have found critical for their very existence. It is not merely coexisting beside another person, with no interaction or relation."[1]

For the next ten days, let's explore what biblical community looks like so that the next time feelings of loneliness threaten to overwhelm us, we'll be equipped from the Scriptures to handle them.

1

The Need for Others

> The LORD God said, "It is not good for the man to be alone. I will make a helper suitable for him."
>
> Genesis 2:18

Carmen's first Christmas as a single mother was incredibly difficult. Happy couples were everywhere—at church, shopping malls, and every party she attended. As the holidays loomed ever nearer, with increasing dread she faced the thought of being alone.

Carmen's struggle with loneliness isn't uncommon for single people.

Singles know Genesis 2:18 well, don't we? We read it, nod our heads in agreement, and ask, "Where is my helper?" and "If it is not good for man to be alone, then why am I?" However, Adam's situation was different from our own because he was the only human being on the planet at the time. He was literally *alone*.

That's not something that we have to experience today. The world is full of people who want contact with others. Sometimes singles think that the only way we can overcome loneliness is to find a spouse. Instead, we should realize that people all around us are seeking connection with someone. While it is certainly possible to feel alone in a crowd, we wouldn't if we were more willing to turn to someone in the crowd and interact.

Churches and many civic groups offer chances to interact with people. Every church I've ever been involved with offers Bible studies and fellowship opportunities. Hospitals, nursing homes, and prisons are full of people who would love to have someone to talk to on a regular basis.

Here's what Carmen did: "My solution was to reach out to other single-parent families and invite them to my home for an open house. Families were invited to stop by between one and five o'clock on Christmas Day and bring something to share. What a great day! People came early and stayed late."

Carmen didn't wait to find a community; she created one.

DIGGING DEEPER INTO GENESIS 2:18

1. List two or three groups or organizations you've considered joining.

2. How often do you initiate conversations with strangers?

3. What barriers do you experience to starting a conversation?

4. Next time you are at a mall or party or anywhere that brings people together, watch how people interact. Find one person who seems relaxed talking with strangers and identify the things he or she says.

5. Name one thing you can do to meet your need for community that would also meet the needs of other singles for community.

2

Finding Community

God sets the lonely in families.

Psalm 68:6

King David knew something about loneliness when he wrote this psalm. In his youth, he was a shepherd. No doubt he spent countless hours in the field without any human contact. Then, after God chose him to be king of Israel, David spent a lot of time on the run from King Saul, who wanted to kill him.

Yet God was at work in David's life long before he first hid from King Saul. After David slew Goliath, King Saul wanted to speak with the young shepherd. When their conversation ended, King Saul's son, Jonathan, became "one in spirit with David, and he loved him as himself" (1 Sam. 18:1). God created a close bond between David and Jonathan that David would rely upon again and again.

Even though David had a family, they wouldn't be able to help him during his loneliest times while hiding from the king. But in God's providence, Jonathan knew King Saul's every move, because he lived with him, and consequently was able to not only keep David safe but also bring him companionship when he needed it the most.

You and I don't live in caves and aren't on the run from a king who wants to take our lives, but we know how it feels to be lonely. Loneliness can make us *feel* as if we live in a cave, as if we are cut off from society and no one cares about our existence. But just as God set David in a family with Jonathan, he does the same for us today.

The apostle Paul said that, as Christians, we have been adopted into God's family (Eph. 1:5). After you've spent ample time with God, your church family is one place that he can use to meet your need for community.

We need to be vulnerable enough in our churches to make close friends and then to lean on one another. God didn't create us to function by ourselves. He created us to rely on him and then each other.

DIGGING DEEPER INTO PSALM 68:6

1. Name all of the Christians in your life whom you consider to be friends.

2. On a scale of 1 to 10, with ten being the highest, how "plugged in" are you with other believers in your church? Explain.

3. List two ways you can invest time and effort in building relationships with people in your church.

4. How and why has your unwillingness to be vulnerable led you to believe that nobody cares, if that is the case?

5. Make this "invite a friend to lunch" week.

3

Wedding Depression

We love Him because He first loved us.

1 John 4:19 NKJV

Weddings. The older we get, the harder it is to avoid feeling lonely as we slide into the pew and watch a friend or relative get married. Gina, a twenty-seven-year-old woman, knows the feeling well. In fact, she and her friends have a name for it: "wedding depression."

Recently, Gina watched a video of a wedding that she appeared in last year, and she felt overwhelmed. "Loneliness just hit me in a wave," Gina said. "I watched the entire video and then ended up on my knees in tears."

You may be able to identify with Gina. I've gone to a movie, watched two characters fall in love, and then, like Gina, been hit by a huge wave of loneliness. God's love for me was the farthest thing from my mind.

Thankfully, God never forgets about his love for us. He was with Gina as she slumped to her knees in tears. He has been with me when I watched two people fall in love on the screen. He is with you whenever you feel alone. His presence and faithfulness call us to recognize and return his love. We don't love God because there is anything good in us that warrants his love. We love God because he first loved us.

Gina knew what she had to do. "I had a good talk with God about what I felt like I needed in my life. God keeps reminding me, as he did in this situation, that he hasn't forgotten about me or my situation, and he is working out the best things in my circumstances."

She also realized another important principle: "If you rely on your spouse/boyfriend/girlfriend to fill the emptiness, then you will spend a good deal of time lonely! Only God can meet those relationship needs to perfection."

DIGGING DEEPER INTO 1 JOHN 4:19

1. Describe your feelings at weddings.

2. Name one friend who would be willing to attend weddings with you in the future.

3. What new tradition, like going to a coffee shop or for a walk in the park, could both of you do after every wedding?

4. Do you ever minimize God's love for you, thinking that his love can't satisfy your needs? If so, describe your thought process.

5. Who is better equipped to meet your every relational need—God or a potential spouse?

4

Knowing Your Neighbors

> Do not forsake your friend and the friend of your father,
> and do not go to your brother's house when disaster
> strikes you—
> better a neighbor nearby than a brother far away.
>
> Proverbs 27:10

In our fast-paced, mobile society, we often move from our hometowns to take jobs in other parts of the country. Nothing is wrong with that, but in recent years, we have also become a suspicious people. We don't trust people we don't know, and we don't know most of our neighbors. Not only do we not know them—we don't even know their names.

Gone are the days when neighbors dropped by with a cake just for the sake of being friendly. The only people we seem to know well are our co-workers, classmates, or fellow church members. All of this suspicion and isolation have come with a cost. With our relatives scattered all over the country, we don't have people close by to turn to during tough times. Or so we think.

The Bible warns us about forsaking friends, and it goes a step further, telling us not to forsake our father's friends. The verse above also implies that we should know our friends and our father's friends so well that we can turn to them when disaster strikes. We always turn to the people closest to us during trying times. If we have spent enough time nurturing friendships before disaster strikes, then we can expect people to be available to help when it comes. Of course, inherent in such an expectation is our willingness to be there in return when disaster strikes our friends' lives.

We have control over who our friends are. We also have control over how much time and effort we put into those friendships. As we meet each other's relational needs, we are better prepared for the tough times of life, because we will face them with people who genuinely care about us.

1. Name your two immediate neighbors. How many other neighbors on your block or in your apartment complex can you name?

2. When you have a problem, who do you call first?

3. List the friends you trust enough to turn to when disaster strikes.

4. List the names of your parents' friends whom you can call.

5. Identify three ways you can meet some of your neighbors this week. Pick one and do it.

5

All I Had Was God

> For I am convinced that neither death nor life, neither angels nor demons, neither the present nor the future, nor any powers, neither height nor depth, nor anything else in all creation, will be able to separate us from the love of God that is in Christ Jesus our Lord.
>
> Romans 8:38–39

Matt is a single, thirty-one-year-old male who serves in the United States military. In January 2000, his brother committed suicide while Matt was in military language school. The school has a no-fraternization policy between officers and enlisted personnel, and because Matt was an officer, he felt isolated during this time of personal grief.

"For six months I went to class half delirious, alone, tired, and soon about to move," Matt said. Because he's in the military, he moves often. His next move took him to Israel. "I never felt more alone, in a culture and land that was so foreign to me. It shocked every part of my system."

In Israel he met a woman and soon fell into the trap many of us do when we are in pain. He sought solace from a member of the opposite sex. He knew he was seeking a woman for the wrong reason, but his pain seemed unbearable alone.

When finding a girlfriend didn't cure his pain and loneliness, he realized something that helped him when he needed it most. "All I had was God, the one who'd been with me my entire life," Matt said. "Only at church—singing, worshiping God, praying, and talking to him—did I get through what proved to be the longest, loneliest time of my life, a stretch of probably a year and a half, before I began to heal."

Matt realized the truth in the Scripture verses above. He discovered that truly *nothing* could separate him from the love of God in Christ Jesus. He discovered that these aren't just nice words to put on a plaque and hang on our wall. Instead, they are words of truth that God uses to call out to us in times of loneliness.

DIGGING DEEPER INTO ROMANS 8:38–39

1. Have you ever sought a relationship because you were going through a trial and didn't want to face it alone? Explain.

2. How did that relationship bring, or fail to bring, the comfort you hoped for?

3. How does God normally satisfy your needs?

4. Describe the last time you felt like Matt did when he said that all he had was God.

5. If you need to tell God that you need him right now, write your prayer below.

6

Single and Forgotten

> At my first defense, no one came to my support, but everyone deserted me. May it not be held against them. But the Lord stood at my side and gave me strength.
>
> 2 Timothy 4:16–17

The apostle Paul faced a defense hearing in a Roman courtroom without anybody at his side. But he wasn't just facing life alone; he was also facing death alone.

Paul knew he was going to die soon (2 Tim. 4:6–7). He wasn't even asking for a stay of execution. He just wanted to be around those he loved. So in verse 9 he asked his understudy, a young pastor named Timothy, to come quickly to visit him. Everyone else but Luke had abandoned him by this point.

Even though his friends were nowhere to be found, God remained with him. God strengthened him so that the Gentiles might hear the gospel. And as much as Paul would have liked to have his friends present, he took great comfort in knowing that God would use his suffering for God's glory.

Sometimes God uses a community of believers to bring us much-needed fellowship. Sometimes he uses a community of just two—"God and me." He has promised never to leave us or forsake us, and we can always count on him to be faithful to his promise. The same God who stood with and strengthened Paul will stand with us and strengthen us as we go about the work that God has given us to do.

Paul could have easily been distracted during his defense hearing because his friends had abandoned him. He could have felt sorry for himself. He could have dashed off a letter to those who had abandoned him. He could have given up. But instead he turned to God, and not only was God glorified but in the process he also gave Paul the fellowship he longed for. God will do the same for us when we turn to him.

1. Think of a traumatic time in your life. How did you handle your feelings?

2. How did your response compare or contrast with Paul's response (he pointed to God's faithfulness to stand with him in v. 17)?

3. Paul wasn't shy about asking his friends to come and visit him when he was unable to go to them. Are you shy about asking for visitors when you need them? Explain.

4. When you are dealing with difficulties, how quickly do you turn to God?

5. Make a list of good things that have happened this week. Start small if you need to. Begin with "a beautiful sunrise" or "my paycheck."

7

A Long Drive

A new command I give you: Love one another. As I have loved you, so you must love one another.

John 13:34

I recently had unexpected minor surgery on one of my big toes. Though the procedure wasn't serious, after the doctor bandaged my toe, I realized that driving home wasn't going to be easy. I could barely fit my foot inside my shoe because the bandage on my toe was so big. Thankfully, my toe was still numb from the Novocain, and after a struggle, I was able to cram my foot inside my shoe.

The doctor handed me a prescription and told me to pick up a few other things at the pharmacy, which is located about five miles from my doctor's office. Maybe it was the "guy" in me showing, but I had not thought about the surgery's aftereffects. So I had not made prior arrangements with a family member or friend to pick me up. Knowing that my family and friends were at work, I didn't want to bother anybody. I started thinking about married friends who have a spouse to help them in similar situations as I drove to the pharmacy by myself. I think it was the loneliest drive I've ever taken.

I should have called one of my family members or friends after the surgery and given them the opportunity to care for me. But I was so caught up in feeling sorry for myself that I totally missed out. My long, lonely drive didn't even need to take place.

I have never found Jesus's command in the above verse—to love one another as he loves us—simple to obey. Allowing someone else to love me as Christ loves me is even more difficult. It means admitting that I need help sometimes with everyday life situations. It means being vulnerable. This event caused me to wonder whether much of the loneliness I feel is unnecessary.

I have a lot of family and friends I could call at any given moment and they would be there—to either help me with something or just listen to me. If I am to be obedient to the command in the verse above, I need to be both a servant to others and the recipient of service from others.

DIGGING DEEPER INTO JOHN 13:34

1. In what circumstances are you generally willing to ask friends or family members for help?

2. How willing do you believe your family or close friends would be if you were to ask them for help?

3. Is it easier for you to show your love for someone else by serving him or her or to receive love from somebody else by his or her service to you? Why?

4. How willing are you to love your family and friends the way you want them to love you?

5. List three people you can call the next time you need help.

8

The God Who Never Fails

The LORD himself goes before you and will be with you;
he will never leave you nor forsake you. Do not be afraid;
do not be discouraged.

Deuteronomy 31:8

As Joshua prepared to take over for Moses in leading the people of Israel into Canaan, Moses knew that Joshua might face discouragement. At times Joshua would feel alone, at times he'd be afraid, and at times he would feel like giving up. Moses had been there himself, but he met face-to-face with God and received all the encouragement he needed to sustain him.

In the presence of all of Israel, Moses tried to pass along to Joshua what he had learned from God by reciting the message in the above verse. Moses saw God go before Israel many times. He saw God send out ten plagues on Egypt in order to persuade Pharaoh to let the Israelites go. He saw God part the Red Sea. He saw God provide manna from heaven when no other food was available.

We aren't told whether Joshua was discouraged, and we aren't told whether he feared the unknown. But no matter how much Moses tried to prepare Joshua for both, surely Joshua struggled with both feelings along the way. He was human, and we all share similar struggles with the unknown.

Just as God went before Israel, he will go before you, reminding you not to be concerned about the future and that he is in control of the present. God is with you today. He is with you as you read this. He is with you as a tear forms in your eye at your sudden awareness of his presence.

He is with you always, and as he promised, he will never leave you or forsake you. Hang on to his promise today as God hangs on to you.

DIGGING DEEPER INTO DEUTERONOMY 31:8

1. Write down one specific way that God has been faithful to meet your need to feel loved and accepted.

2. What did God do differently than you expected when he met the need described in the previous question?

3. Do you believe that God will be with you in the midst of your struggles with loneliness, just as he was with Joshua? Explain.

4. How confident are you that God will be with you in your fear of facing the future alone?

5. What can you do to make sure you hang on to God's promise that he will never leave you or forsake you (e.g., writing down and carrying a Scripture verse with you or memorizing a verse)?

9

Spurring Each Other On

> And let us consider how we may spur one another on toward love and good deeds. Let us not give up meeting together, as some are in the habit of doing, but let us encourage one another—and all the more as you see the Day approaching.
>
> Hebrews 10:24–25

Marriage doesn't necessarily cure loneliness. Listen to a fifty-eight-year-old woman named Kathy: "I struggled with loneliness even when I was with my spouse," she said. "I would attend social functions with my co-workers, and I would never tell my husband he was invited, because he would drink too much and embarrass me. But then I would be lonely at these functions because everyone else was with a spouse and I wasn't. I longed to be just like the rest of them."

Kathy moved in with her son after separating from her husband, but that didn't cure her feelings of loneliness either. "I was very lonely for the first few weeks and constantly prayed for the Lord to help me find a new church home," she said. God answered her prayer.

Kathy went to the right place for help. Look again at the passage above from Hebrews 10. When the body of Christ meets, we are to consider how we may spur one another on toward love and good deeds. God's people are supposed to be continually meeting and helping one another in their service to God. In return, the interaction and love we receive from them satisfies our longing to be accepted, appreciated, and loved.

The writer of Hebrews knew that if we forsook church, we would miss out on the closeness that comes only when we are active in the body of Christ. If you need a community, get involved in the lives of people at church. Don't wait for them to invite you to a church outing or Bible study; you invite them. Show concern for others, and many of them will show concern for you in return.

DIGGING DEEPER INTO HEBREWS 10:24–25

1. Have you ever thought that simply getting married would cure your feelings of loneliness? Explain.

2. How often do you attend church, Sunday school or small group, and social gatherings at your church?

3. What is the correlation between the amount of time, or lack thereof, that you invest in other believers at church and your sense of community?

4. What activity have you considered starting or getting involved with at church but for some reason have hesitated? Why?

5. In the context of Hebrews 10:24, how might the Lord use this activity and your involvement with it to spur church members toward love and good deeds?

10

The Soothing Sound
of a Gentle Whisper

> Then a great and powerful wind tore the mountains apart
> and shattered the rocks before the LORD, but the LORD
> was not in the wind. After the wind there was an earth-
> quake, but the LORD was not in the earthquake. After the
> earthquake came a fire, but the LORD was not in the fire.
> And after the fire came a gentle whisper.
>
> 1 Kings 19:11–12

After Elijah executed 450 prophets of Baal in the Brook Kishon (1 Kings 18:40), King Ahab told his wife, Jezebel, about the prophet's act. By this point, she had already successfully turned Ahab into a Baal worshiper, so she was infuriated with Elijah.

Elijah escaped into the wilderness and was in such despair that he asked God to take his life. Instead, God sent an angel to feed and watch out for him during his time of distress. Then God decided to visit Elijah. God could have shown up in the wind, in an earthquake, or in fire, but he chose to appear to Elijah in a gentle whisper.

Just as God was with Elijah as he feared for his life alone in the wilderness, he is with us. But it is easy to miss him in our noisy world. We read stories in the Bible about how God gloriously manifested himself to the saints of old in a visible fashion, and sometimes we long for that kind of attention from him. Yet God's whisper to Elijah was just as glorious as his other chosen methods of manifestation and even a bit more intimate.

Whispers bring comfort. Remember when you used to skin your knee as a child and go running to Mom? After she doctored you, she whispered, "Shhh. Everything's going to be all right." And it was. God gave mothers a voice designed to bring comfort to their children.

Are you taking the time to listen to God's gentle whisper? It's often the way God speaks to us, but we've got to settle the wind, earthquakes, and fires in our lives long enough to hear him.

DIGGING DEEPER INTO 1 KINGS 19:11–12

1. God spoke to Elijah in a whisper. What ways does God speak to us?

2. When was the last time God whispered to you?

3. Describe the intimacy you felt with God during that experience.

4. What did God say to you?

5. What do you need to tune out so you can hear God's whisper now?

Part 2

Completeness

If you are like most other singles, you've spent your share of time couple watching. They walk hand in hand, seemingly oblivious to their surroundings, and yet at the same time, they seem to bring their surroundings to life.

What happens to your emotions when you watch couples? Beyond your yearning for love is a sense of incompleteness. If you just had what those couples had, you'd feel as if you could be the person God wants you to be.

As Christians, we know that we are complete in Christ. We've read the Scripture verses and heard the sermons, especially from singles pastors, that clearly tell us we are complete in Christ without a spouse. Why, then, don't our feelings match what our heads already know?

The primary reason we struggle with this question is likely because we incorrectly conclude that because God gives most of us a desire to be accepted and loved by a person of the opposite sex, we must be incomplete if we don't have someone to love. Our worth or sense of completeness comes from acceptance and love from the opposite sex, or lack thereof, rather than from God.

God never intended our sense of value or completeness to come from another person. No man or woman can love you the way God can. No man or woman can complete you the way God can. No man or woman can satisfy the desires of your heart the way God can.

In part 5, we will deal with the concept of longing for love in-depth, but before we get there, you need to know something: Longing for love isn't wrong. In fact, it is often the mechanism that God uses to bring two people together to form a marriage. However, feeling as if you're less of a person in the midst of your longing is wrong.

For the next ten days, the Bible will show us what completeness in Christ looks like. Are you willing to let the Scriptures speak to your feelings of incompleteness? If so, don't be surprised at what God does with your feelings.

11

Five Marriages Later

> Jesus answered her, "If you knew the gift of God and who it is that asks you for a drink, you would have asked him and he would have given you living water."
>
> John 4:10

After Jesus sat down by Jacob's well in Sychar, a local Samaritan woman came to the well to gather water. He asked her for a drink, and she was astonished that Jesus would even associate with her. Jews didn't see Samaritans as true worshipers of God, because Samaritans were a mixed race. Jewish men also didn't speak with women in public. Jesus crossed both lines in asking this woman for a drink.

Jesus's response to her astonishment is given in the verse above. After his answer, she expressed an interest in the living water that Jesus told her about—thinking that he just meant that she could receive an endless supply of physical water. Jesus then told her to get her husband and come back to the well. She told him the truth, that she had no husband. Jesus again surprised her by telling her he knew she had had five husbands and that the man she was with was not number six.

Imagine her shame. She already felt incomplete because she was a Samaritan and a woman. To also have Jesus point out her current sin must have made her feel even worse. But notice that Jesus never treated her as incomplete. He ignored her heritage and the fact that she was a woman. He also didn't consider her less of a person or more of a person just because she had been married multiple times and was in a sinful relationship.

If marriage makes a person complete, then this woman was five times as complete as the person who has never married. Obviously that is not the case. Instead, Jesus pointed to the one thing she was missing—living water. In the Old Testament, living water was a sign that God was at work (see Jer. 2:13 and Zech. 14:8). She was missing God's work in her life—salvation. As she drank of the living water, she tapped into the only source that can truly make people complete.

DIGGING DEEPER INTO JOHN 4:10

1. What is the source of your feelings of incompleteness?

2. Do you feel incomplete before people, God, or both? Explain.

3. Did Jesus treat the Samaritan woman as if she was incomplete? Explain.

4. Do you think that the woman was five times as complete as someone who's never been married? Why or why not?

5. How can the living water that Jesus spoke about be the only thing that can make a person complete?

12

The Perfect Spouse

For your Maker is your husband.

Isaiah 54:5

Paul is a single, twenty-six-year-old office worker who knows quite a bit about his co-workers' personal lives. He knows who is married, who is in a relationship, and who is single. He is bothered sometimes knowing that he faces an empty house after a long, hard day at work, while some of his co-workers go home to a spouse.

We often think that couples get along perfectly and that each is available for the other at a moment's notice. But is that really the case or just our idealization? We've romanticized marriage so much that we don't think about obvious realities married couples face. Like us, they too have church responsibilities, work responsibilities, bills to pay, parents to care for, groceries to buy, and often, children to tend to.

Paul figured out what to do after one especially long, hard day at the office: "The only thing I could do was pray." It was the best thing Paul could have done, because it started him on a journey that led him to a truth that helped him deal with his false sense of incompleteness. "I learned to talk to God as though he were my wife. I learned that I could trust God and he could fill the role of a wife. Someone who would listen, patiently wait, and respond with answers of love."

According to Isaiah 54:5, as believers we are married to God. How many of us have neglected our first and most important love by not nurturing our relationship with him? He's a perfect spouse, with ample time to listen, and he understands us better than we understand ourselves.

1. Describe how you felt the last time you thought about others going home from work to their spouses.

2. When you imagine going home to a spouse after a hard day, do you ever think about that spouse being distracted without much time for a long conversation that day? Explain.

3. When you've read or heard Isaiah 54:5 in the past, what were your perceptions about God being your spouse?

4. How has thinking about the ramifications of this verse given you a better perspective about what it means to have God as a spouse?

5. If you have neglected God, what can you do to get back on track in your marriage with him?

13

Our Unknown God

For in him we live and move and have our being.

Acts 17:28

When the apostle Paul visited Athens, he was grieved to find the city full of idols. He recognized that the people of Athens were religious but still separated from God. He began to reveal the one true God to them by telling them that God doesn't dwell in temples and that from one man he made every nation on earth—even going so far as to say that God determined the exact times and places that people would live throughout all of history. Then he told them the reason God did this—so people would seek him (Acts 17:27).

Paul continued by telling them that God wasn't far from them, and that in reality it is only because of him that they were alive and able to do anything. A few people became followers of Jesus that day. I suspect that Paul's message appealed to them because they had long worshiped an unknown god (Acts 17:23), and when they heard about the God who cared enough about people to be involved in their everyday lives—right down to the places they lived—they wanted to worship such a God. They repented of their sin and entered into fellowship with a God who wants to be known.

What wishes and desires have we made into an unknown god? A career move? A spouse? A car? A new home? Completeness in Christ and purpose in life don't depend on any of those things.

Paul would tell us that God isn't far from us and that we can find completeness only in him. Because of *God*, we live. Without his sustaining hand, we would cease to breathe.

Because of God, we move. Jesus said that we can do nothing apart from him. Because of God, we have our being. How much more complete could we possibly be?

DIGGING DEEPER INTO ACTS 17:28

1. What desires have you made into an unknown god?

2. What needs have you been hoping those desires would meet that only God can truly meet?

3. Have you ever felt as if you had no purpose in life? Explain.

4. If God loves you so much that he goes so far as to determine the exact place you live, how much more do you think he cares about your need to feel complete?

5. Do you need to repent for making some desire into an unknown god? If so, write your prayer of repentance here.

14

The Company Picnic Blues

What is more, I consider everything a loss compared to the surpassing greatness of knowing Christ Jesus my Lord, for whose sake I have lost all things. I consider them rubbish, that I may gain Christ and be found in him.

Philippians 3:8–9

Company picnics and other after-hour company social gatherings have been a struggle for me. I don't like to attend social gatherings alone. One year only a few of my co-workers from my department showed up at the annual company picnic, and sure enough, I ended up alone.

I went through the food line, and as I did I glanced around the picnic area, searching for a place to sit. I didn't know many of the people there because I worked for a big company, so I finally decided to sit by myself. Eventually a few employees from other departments joined me, but most of them came and went as I sat there alone.

Then came the dance. As I watched couples flood the dance floor, they got lost in each other's presence. They fed off each other. One would lean in close to whisper something to the other, drawing laughter, a smile, or giggles. I never felt so incomplete.

I was in a funk for several days after the picnic. I couldn't stop thinking about how incomplete I felt. I knew in my mind that I was complete in Christ, but my emotions didn't seem to care. In fact, they objected. What I failed to realize at the time was that my emotions can and often are manipulated by circumstances—like the picnic—but they have nothing to do with whether I am complete in God's eyes.

If I had considered everything a loss—including someone to whisper to on a dance floor—compared to the greatness of knowing Jesus Christ, as the apostle Paul said in the above verse, my emotions would not have gotten the best of me. Sage advice from a man who refused to be governed by his emotions.

DIGGING DEEPER INTO PHILIPPIANS 3:8-9

1. Describe the feelings you had the last time you attended an event and felt incomplete without somebody by your side.

2. How did you deal with your emotions? Did you let them overwhelm you like I did?

3. How long did it take for you to remember that your completeness as a person comes only from your relationship with Christ?

4. Can you honestly say that you consider everything as rubbish compared to knowing Jesus? Explain.

5. Do your actions reflect that you count everything else as rubbish? Are you spending time in prayer, reading your Bible, and relying on him during your daily routines?

15

One in Christ Jesus

> You are all sons of God through faith in Christ Jesus, for all of you who were baptized into Christ have clothed yourselves with Christ. There is neither Jew nor Greek, slave nor free, male nor female, for you are all one in Christ Jesus.
>
> Galatians 3:26–28

As the apostle Paul laid out his case to the church in Galatia that people are saved by faith and not the law, he made the above statement. He wanted the Galatians to know that one person wasn't better or more favored in God's sight than anyone else who placed his or her faith in Christ—a fact that seems obvious to us, but it wasn't then. Jews were God's chosen people, and the thought of allowing Gentiles into the church without them living up to the demands of the law seemed unthinkable.

Paul didn't want that error to continue in the church. He wanted everybody to see one another as united with Christ, not as Jewish or Greek, slave or free, male or female. Heritage didn't matter. Gender didn't matter. Social status didn't matter. Their faith made them all one in Christ Jesus.

Jesus is an equal opportunity redeemer. He doesn't do it because we deserve it or because we are better than other people but simply because he loves us. He not only redeems us but gives us new life with the promise that he will never leave us.

He seeks us out for fellowship. He freely gives us wisdom as we go about our daily routine if we just ask for it. He calms our troubled souls when we feel overwhelmed by life. He brings people into our lives to help us when we need it. He protects our lives. He gives us jobs by which to provide for us. He gives us good Christian friends who encourage us in the faith. He does countless other things for us because of our union with him.

Imagine living without his presence, his guidance, his encouragement, his Word, his church, his protection, and his provision. How much different would your life be if you were not united with Jesus? Thankfully you will never have to find out.

DIGGING DEEPER INTO GALATIANS 3:26–28

1. Why does the gospel cross all lines of heritage, gender, and social status?

2. If God saves us because he loves us and not because we are deserving of salvation, what should that do to the notions of racism, sexism, and classism?

3. Do you consider single missionaries, single church planters, or other single servants who went before us to be incomplete? Explain.

4. List five things that God has done for you as a result of your union with him.

5. How would your life be different if you were not a Christian?

16

God-Given Satisfaction

> When I was woven together in the depths of the earth,
>   your eyes saw my unformed body.
> All the days ordained for me
>   were written in your book
>   before one of them came to be.
>
> Psalm 139:15–16

I love to read stories about how God uses singles. One of my favorite stories comes from a book by Harold Ivan Smith titled *Movers & Shapers: Singles Who Changed Their World*. One chapter is about a single woman named Henrietta Mears who was born in 1890 and died in 1961.

When Mears became the director of Christian education at her church, she reviewed the curriculum and determined that it was not adequate to reach the children; it was missing illustrations, didn't account for children at different age levels (they all used the same material), and jumped all over the Bible rather than teaching sequentially.

When two children told her they were not getting anything out of the material, with permission from her pastor, Mears began to write her own curriculum for each age level. She pieced her writing together with pictures from old religious calendars and copied the material for the children to use. The curriculum made an immediate impact on the children, and word spread about its effectiveness.

She eventually found a printer, and these books began the Gospel Light Publishing Company. Within a decade, a quarter of a million books had been sold. It all started when one single woman desired to meet the needs of spiritually malnourished children at her church. Years later, she reflected, "Through one experience after another the Lord has shown me that He had something peculiar and special for me to do. After I went through that final door, where it was just the Lord and myself, I've gone into wide open spaces of people and things and excitement, and life has been an adventure. It has been a tremendous thing to see how the Lord has filled my life so abundantly."[2]

Henrietta Mears found what her "days were ordained for," as Psalm 139 says. By being faithful to do what she knew to be right, she felt so complete that she called her life with God an "adventure" and said that he had filled her life with "abundance."

DIGGING DEEPER INTO PSALM 139:15-16

1. What needs at your church has God equipped you to meet?

2. How faithful have you been to meet them?

3. What primary task has God ordained for your days?

4. How abundant does your life currently feel?

5. How has God spoken to you through this passage?

17

The Satisfaction of Spiritual Maturity

> Perseverance must finish its work so that you may be mature and complete, not lacking anything.
>
> James 1:4

God intends for his followers to be mature in the faith. All of us who claim the name of Christ are on a journey toward that goal. On that journey, we will encounter "many trials," which God uses to develop perseverance in us (James 1:2–3). Notice that God's part of the equation is to bring or allow trials into our lives. How we respond to those trials has a direct result upon our maturity level in the faith.

We can imitate the believers in the book of Hebrews (Heb. 5:11–14) who were still drinking milk, or we can become mature like the believers who ate solid food. Those of us who are still drinking milk—who have never spent much time in the Word of God—will never feel satisfied or "complete." Those who have moved to solid food—through regular and intense Bible study—realize that circumstances, no matter what they are, have nothing to do with their sense of completeness.

As we start each day in the Word, we prepare ourselves for the trials that will come our way. I always see a direct correlation between the time I spend in the Word and the way I handle trials. If my study time is short or nonexistent, my mind is not fixed on the things of God, and I react out of my sin nature. If my study time is regular and deep, my mind is constantly processing trials from a biblical perspective as I try to discern the most biblical reaction.

44

During those spiritually dry periods in my life, I feel weak, unmotivated to stay in the Scriptures, and incomplete. God has always been faithful to challenge me not to neglect my duty to "study to show myself approved" (2 Tim. 2:15). During times of intense study, I feel spiritually and mentally strong. I feel as if I'm living with purpose. I feel I'm in God's will. I also feel so full of God that I couldn't possibly be more complete.

DIGGING DEEPER INTO JAMES 1:4

1. If you had to give yourself a grade from 1 to 10 based upon how spiritually mature you are right now, what would it be and why?

2. How do you define spiritual maturity?

3. How does your definition line up with James 1:4?

4. How does your spiritual maturity directly affect your sense of completeness?

5. List two things you can do to minimize the frequency of spiritual dry periods in your life.

18

He Loved the Unlovely

> But because of his great love for us, God, who is rich in
> mercy, made us alive with Christ even when we were dead
> in transgressions—it is by grace you have been saved.
>
> Ephesians 2:4–5

God is the only one who can meet our needs, understand us completely, and love us without condition.
Look at the verse above. Because of his great love for us,
he made us alive in Christ even when we were dead in our
sin. We were filthy, wretched sinners without the ability to
hide our sin from his sight.

Think about some of your worst sins—the ones you
wouldn't tell anyone about, at least not right away. Why?
Because you are afraid that you would be rejected, aren't
you? God knew about all of those sins and all of the sins
that you will ever commit. He loved you anyway, enough to
send his Son to die a horrible, painful death to prove it.

He breathed eternal life into your dead lungs, raised you
in Christ, and seated you with him in the heavenly realms
(Eph. 2:6). This isn't figurative language. Jesus promised to
prepare a specific place for us in heaven (John 14:2). The
seat in heaven that the apostle Paul spoke of in Ephesians
2:6 is ours by right because of Jesus. In 1 Corinthians 6:2–3,
Paul goes on to say that you and I will judge the world and
the angels. I can't even comprehend this privilege God has
given us.

I know only that God desires his church to be with him
for eternity. All of the joy you and I receive from worshiping God in church right now is but a glimpse of what is
to come. If a group of people should feel as complete as

humans can feel, it is the church. Only when we fail to set our minds on the things above do we forget God's love for us and that he has destined us for a future beyond anything we can imagine.

1. When was the last time you needed to feel loved without condition?

2. If you were able to find it, describe how that felt.

3. What comes to your mind when you think about being seated in the heavenly realms with Jesus?

4. Look up John 14:2; 1 Corinthians 6:2–3; and Ephesians 2:6. Describe the sense of God's love you feel after reading these passages.

5. How have these verses changed your perspective about your sense of completeness?

19

Guilty of the Unthinkable

> For in Him [Christ] dwells all the fullness of the Godhead
> bodily; and you are complete in Him, who is the head of
> all principality and power.
>
> Colossians 2:9–10 NKJV

As the apostle Paul sought to warn believers in the Colosse church about false teachers who taught a "works" salvation. He made it clear to them that redemption can be found only in Jesus (Col. 1:13–14). He also wanted believers in Colosse to know they were complete in Christ. They weren't complete because they did all the right things, said all the right things, or hung out with the right people. They were complete in Christ because they placed their faith in Jesus, God in the flesh, who died for their sins.

Paul didn't want them longing for completeness in anything or anyone else. To do so would take away from the finished work of Jesus on the cross. It would say that faith in the one who is the head of all principality and power, who is indwelt with all the fullness of the godhead, wasn't enough to complete them. What a tragedy for the Colosse church that would have been.

I wonder how close we are to making the same mistake. We don't intend to trample on the work of Christ on the cross as the only way for humans to truly be complete, but by insinuating that we are incomplete, for whatever reason, we may be guilty of doing the unthinkable.

With Christ as our foundation—and a growing, vibrant spiritual life that seeks fulfillment only in him—we experience a sense of completeness. So rather than exhausting ourselves trying to feel complete by some external desire, let's rest in the fact that he's already found us.

DIGGING DEEPER INTO COLOSSIANS 2:9–10

1. When you read Scripture passages that say you are complete in Christ, what is your first thought?

2. How have you exhausted yourself trying to find the right activity or the right person to feel complete?

3. Have you ever thought that believing you are incomplete demeans Jesus's work on the cross? Explain.

4. How do you need to stop trying to obtain a sense of completeness?

5. What do you need to do to recognize your completeness in Christ?

20

In God's Likeness

> Then God said, "Let us make man in our image, in our likeness, and let them rule over the fish of the sea and the birds of the air, over the livestock, over all the earth, and over all the creatures that move along the ground."
>
> Genesis 1:26

After God finished creating the heavens and the earth, he filled the earth with land, vegetation, sea creatures, birds, and animals. Then he created man—the only thing he created in his image—and gave him dominion over the rest of his creation.

Does that story still take your breath away? It should. The God of the universe knew we would betray him soon, but he chose to make us in his image anyway. Then he entrusted us with the rest of his creation. Talk about a purpose!

As humans we tend to forget what God did for us yesterday, let alone what he did for humankind at creation. Without a constant reminder that God made us and gave us a purpose, we seldom think that way. We think about our needs, our hurts, and how we can stay entertained. Thankfully, the Scriptures and other Christians challenge us to move beyond ourselves and find our purpose.

We act as if God's shaping us in his image and entrusting us with his creation is a fairy tale. If caring for his creation weren't enough, Jesus also told us to take the gospel to the nations and adhere to all of his teachings—the ones that tell us to love each other, pray for each other, and tend to each other's needs.

If you want to feel complete, first remind yourself that you are made in God's image. Second, do what he told you to do. Be a good steward of all he's given you. Share the Good News with someone. Lend a helping hand to those in need. Feelings of completeness will follow.

1. Have you ever considered the fact that you are made in the image of God and therefore you knock his work when you say you are incomplete?

2. God knew every sin that we would ever commit, and he chose to make us in his image anyway. How does this change the way you think about your completeness?

3. If you were to share the Good News and help those in need more often, how do you think your struggle with feeling incomplete would be affected?

4. What or who have you spent the most time thinking about this past week? Do you think those thoughts play into your struggle with feelings of incompleteness?

5. Name at least one thing you plan to do this week to share the gospel with a friend or help someone in need.

Part 3

Emotional Health

All of us want to be emotionally healthy. We would rather not have to deal with failed relationships or marriages and the hurtful words that often result from them. We would rather not have to deal with the death of a parent, the loss of a job, or the difficulties that come from growing up in a home where one or both parents were substance abusers.

But most of us will experience failed relationships prior to marriage, and some of us have already faced the painful difficulty of divorce. Most of us will face the death of our parents if the Lord wills that we outlive them. Most of us will go through multiple jobs. Some of us struggle with our self-image. Some of us will have to learn to overcome a poor upbringing.

These are the cycles of life. The experiences are different, but all of us will undergo change and loss. One common response is to withdraw from life, feeling as if nobody else has ever endured such painful circumstances. Instead, the first step toward healing is recognizing that we're not the only ones who've faced a particular difficulty.

This section is not designed to give you advice in dealing with mental illnesses or chemical imbalances. If you, or somebody you trust, suspect that you have either one, you should seek help from a professional immediately. Part 3 is about maintaining good emotional health in spite of losing people, relationships, jobs, or anything else we love or enjoy.

We cannot avoid difficult stretches of life, for they will come. Rather, we will focus on what to do when they arrive. How do we obtain and maintain good emotional health so we can do the things God wants us to do right now and so we can be prepared for the future?

For the next ten days, we will examine the Scriptures about good emotional health, the healing power of Jesus Christ, and what a redeemed future looks like.

21

Sticks and Stones Are Nothing Compared to Words

> When they hurled their insults at him, he did not retaliate; when he suffered, he made no threats. Instead, he entrusted himself to him who judges justly.
>
> 1 Peter 2:23

I don't know who came up with "Sticks and stones may break my bones, but words will never hurt me," but I often wonder if he or she ever experienced harsh, unloving words meant to cut into a person's soul.

When Gail was struggling to leave a relationship that she knew she should never have begun, her father spoke such words: "No man will ever want you. You will never get married." She never forgot them. Even a deserved rebuke spoken by a family member or friend should never be so harsh.

"These words spoken by my father haunted me," Gail said. "They stood in the shadows and laughed at the brokenness of my femininity. I drifted through a sea of unhealthy relationships, never docking at stability's safe harbor. Rejection was my life's anchor, loneliness my perverted ally."

Words have a tremendous amount of power, in spite of the old *sticks and stones* adage. As Christians, we base our entire lives on the Word of God. Jesus is the Word incarnate. Words kept Gail from experiencing life the way God intended.

Have you ever been on the receiving end of words that tore into your soul? Can you still remember the exact words spoken? Have you ever recovered from them? Would you like to recover? Follow Christ's example on the cross.

He entrusted himself to him who judges justly. The Gospel accounts of his crucifixion go one step further than 1 Peter 2:23 and say that Jesus asked the Father to forgive those who put him to death. He didn't ignore the insults or even claim that they didn't hurt, but he also didn't shout insults in return. By turning to the Father, he found compassion for those who were about to kill him.

DIGGING DEEPER INTO 1 PETER 2:23

1. Has anybody ever spoken sharp words to you that you can still recall verbatim? Who was it and what did he or she say?

2. How have you dealt with that comment?

3. How does the way you handled it compare or contrast with the way Jesus did in 1 Peter 2:23?

4. What can you do to change the way you've dealt with those harmful words to make your response more like Jesus's?

5. Can you say that you've found compassion for the person who hurt you? If not, meditate on this passage and ask God to give you a heart like Jesus had for his killers.

22

Just the Way You Are

> The LORD said to him, "Who gave man his mouth? Who makes him deaf or mute? Who gives him sight or makes him blind? Is it not I, the LORD? Now go; I will help you speak and will teach you what to say."
>
> Exodus 4:11–12

If you love to read old literature, you are familiar with the way great authors differentiate between people who are beautiful and people who are "plain." Our culture is not so kind as to use the word "plain" for those it deems so. And beyond physical appearance, it is also not so kind to those it deems different in any fashion, such as those from a different socioeconomic class or those with shyness problems, speech impediments, or physical or mental challenges.

Moses knew how inadequacy felt. After God told Moses to go to the Israelites and tell them that God had chosen him to lead them out of bondage in Egypt (Exodus 3), Moses was afraid they would not believe him. He argued with God for a while, and then he said, "O Lord, I have never been eloquent, neither in the past nor since you have spoken to your servant. I am slow of speech and tongue" (4:10).

Though this was one excuse in a list of excuses that Moses used to try to avoid what God wanted him to do, what he said was apparently true, because as angry as this excuse made God (v. 14), God told Moses to let his brother, Aaron, do the talking to Israel because Aaron could speak well (v. 14).

God created Moses's mouth, and he chooses to create other people with what modern culture would call "deficiencies." If you struggle with a poor self-image for any reason, you can take comfort in knowing that God created you just the way you are. And as God promised to help Moses speak, God will help you do exactly what he wants you to do.

DIGGING DEEPER INTO EXODUS 4:11–12

1. Name one aspect of your physical makeup or personality about which you are insecure.

2. How has this aspect stopped you from living a healthy life?

3. Have you ever used it as an excuse not to serve God in an area he led you to?

4. Why do you think God created people with different strengths and weaknesses?

5. How might God use your insecurity for his glory?

23

Daddy's Gone

> When you pass through the waters,
>   I will be with you;
> and when you pass through the rivers,
>   they will not sweep over you.
>
>   Isaiah 43:2

Daddy's gone." My sister always called him Daddy, even though the day he died she was thirty years old.

My sister's words stunned me. I went numb as I walked to my car from work after receiving her phone call. The numbness turned to sharp, piercing pain on the trip to my sister's house where Dad was. An overwhelming sense of loss swept over me. I thought about never hearing his voice on the phone again asking me to play golf or asking my opinion of the latest political news. I thought about never being able to talk to him again about his new faith in Christ.

Less than a year before his death, after much witnessing by one of his friends at work and by me, he told me he believed in Christ. After asking him a few questions, I had little doubt that his faith was genuine. I wanted to revel in that thought on the way to my sister's house, but my sense of loss won the battle that day.

During his funeral, I cried tears of mourning *and* rejoicing. In the following days, my tears continued as I sorted through his things with my siblings. As the days turned into weeks and the weeks into months, I sensed God's presence as I seldom have in other circumstances because I counted on him to take me through the waters, as Isaiah 43:2 says. As I did so, God kept the rivers from sweeping me away in despair.

God knows how it feels to lose a loved one. He watched as his Son was beaten beyond recognition and nailed to a cross so that sinners might live. If you have lost someone you love and you are a Christian, you are not alone. God is ready to walk with you through pain's sharpest pierces. Lean into him as he walks with you.

DIGGING DEEPER INTO ISAIAH 43:2

1. Have you ever been overwhelmed with a sense of loss by the death of a parent, family member, or close friend? Write his or her name here.

2. Describe your emotions during that difficult time.

3. Did you feel you endured your mourning alone, or did you sense God's presence?

4. In what ways can God be close to us during trying times, as in the death of a loved one?

5. What can you do to sense his presence during times of mourning?

24

Recovering from Bad Choices

> Therefore, there is now no condemnation for those who
> are in Christ Jesus, because through Christ Jesus the law
> of the Spirit of life set me free from the law of sin and
> death.
>
> Romans 8:1–2

Bad choices. We've all made them. Brett is no exception. He was with a woman who didn't share his faith, and as a result, their different worldviews pulled them apart. When Brett went on a short-term mission trip with YWAM (Youth With A Mission), a friend on the mission field pointed out the reason for the failed relationship.

"Then, when I got home and saw my ex-girlfriend, all that advice flew out the window," Brett said. "I spent most of the next year trying to get her to go out with me again, and it was very emotionally unhealthy for me."

During that year, Brett was accountable to friends, but his friends didn't do what is necessary in accountability relationships—they weren't willing to lovingly but strongly tell him that he was off base. "I just wanted to hear them say no, and they didn't, so I carried on with it," Brett said.

Brett knew that his friends weren't the reason he couldn't walk away from the relationship, but he felt too weak to make the decision himself. Beyond his attempts to be in a relationship that he knew wasn't right, he felt guilty for the physical compromises in the relationship when they were together. One bad choice led to another. They always do.

Recovering from bad decisions isn't easy—it usually is a process. In Brett's case, several things finally helped him. First, he found people at YWAM whom he could trust, and he confessed his sin to them. Second, he asked his former girlfriend to forgive him for the way he had treated her and for the compromises he had asked her to make. Finally, he clung to the verse above.

The road to good emotional health for Brett was paved by confession, repentance, and the knowledge that God did not condemn him.

DIGGING DEEPER INTO ROMANS 8:1-2

1. How do your choices influence your emotional health?

2. How have you tried to improve your emotional health?

3. What did you do with your guilt over the poor choice(s) you made?

4. To whom have you made yourself accountable so that you do not repeat your poor choices or continue down that road?

5. If you have repented for your poor choice(s), what are you doing to avoid the sense of condemnation that Satan tries to convince you to embrace?

25

Run to the Refuge

> You have been a refuge for the poor,
> a refuge for the needy in his distress,
> a shelter from the storm
> and a shade from the heat.
> For the breath of the ruthless
> is like a storm driving against a wall
> and like the heat of the desert.
>
> Isaiah 25:4–5

The aftermath of a hurricane brings stillness, a sense of awe, and the overwhelming sense of loss. You've seen video of the demolished houses, cars turned upside down, and personal photos scattered for blocks. You've seen the distress of those who view their loss up close for the first time.

Isaiah paints such a picture for us in the above verses. The difference is that he is talking about the type of storms that people bring into our lives. Whether between family, friends, or co-workers, you know how quickly harsh words can be tossed into the air, never to be taken back. The initial sting hurts the heart, but the lasting effect is felt by the soul.

In this passage Isaiah praised God for being a refuge for the needy who are in distress. When you are distressed because of a storm of words hurled your way, do you take refuge in God? Is he the shade that protects you from the heat?

The Hebrew word for "shelter" in verse 4 above means "a fortified place." It's a place nobody can penetrate. It's a place where wounds are tended and allowed to heal. It's a place of safety.

Christians have access to God as their fortress because his Spirit dwells within us. However, that does not mean we always willingly go into the shelter. Sometimes we seek refuge elsewhere—in friends, in church, and from the things of this world. While friends and the church are good places to find comfort, only one place can truly provide a place of safety and nurturing until we are well again. Run to the place of refuge. Run to God.

DIGGING DEEPER INTO ISAIAH 25:4-5

1. In the past, when you heard or read about God being your refuge in times of trouble, what did that mean to you?

2. In what ways can God be your refuge during stormy times?

3. Where do you normally turn when you need a place of refuge?

4. On your list of importance, when it comes to finding a place of refuge, where does God normally rank?

5. If God has not been first on your list, write a prayer of confession here.

26

The Good Ol' Days

> But one thing I do: Forgetting what is behind and strain-
> ing toward what is ahead, I press on toward the goal to
> win the prize for which God has called me heavenward
> in Christ Jesus.
>
> Philippians 3:13–14

The apostle Paul was in prison when he wrote his letter to the Philippians. Yet that didn't stop him from being excited about his future, even though he seemed to know that his future here on earth would soon end. The Roman world wouldn't tolerate his message much longer.

Think about how easy it would have been for Paul to dwell on the past while sitting in prison. He was born a Jew—he descended from the tribe of Benjamin, was cir-cumcised on the eighth day, became a Pharisee, and was well-versed in God's law. Those around him viewed him in high esteem. He was in authority. He was in control. He easily could have fallen into the trap of considering those the "good ol' days."

As he wrote to the church in Philippi, he made it clear that he not only avoided that trap but that his mind was set on the future—the eternal. He also didn't let the good ol' days stop him from doing what needed to be done in the present. He preached the gospel, knowing that it could and probably would cost him his life here on earth.

Your good ol' days might consist of high school friends left behind, prowess in athletics, a dream job that never materialized, or a relationship that never worked out. Life in the present never seems as sweet as "what might have been."

Paul left his past in the past with a specific goal in mind: heaven. It wasn't easy for him. Notice that the verses above say he *strained* "toward what is ahead" and he *pressed on*. He changed his focus from all that he might have missed to the prize of heaven. In light of heaven, his good ol' days didn't carry the same allure as they might have otherwise.

DIGGING DEEPER INTO PHILIPPIANS 3:13–14

1. Name something or someone from your past that you can't quit thinking about.

2. What have you done to try to leave this person, dream, or event in your past?

3. How successful have you been?

4. If you were to spend more time thinking about your future in heaven, how might that change the way you think about the past?

5. If the apostle Paul had to "strain toward what is ahead," then you will too. Name one thing you can do today to strain toward your life in heaven.

27

Trusting God for Employment

Cast your cares on the LORD
and he will sustain you;
he will never let the righteous fall.

Psalm 55:22

Corporate America is not what it used to be. Neither are today's employees. Gone are the days when companies hired employees in their late teens or early twenties and promoted them up the ladder over the next several decades. Gone are the days when employees felt a sense of loyalty to their employers.

As technology advanced and dot-com companies came and went, companies fought for survival with smaller staffs than sometimes necessary. Many employees soon found themselves out of work with every downturn in the economy. So the sense of loyalty on both sides is now understandably less than it once was.

Such a business climate makes it difficult to feel financially secure on a long-term basis as workers once did. Each time we are downsized, the stress to find a new position as soon as possible increases.

We have to take the blame for some of that stress. We don't save enough money for times of emergency, and too many of us live a lifestyle we can't afford. A quick inventory of our CDs, DVDs, magazine subscriptions, clothing, and book collections would probably affirm that we spend too much money entertaining ourselves.

Beyond the stress that we bring on ourselves for not being financially responsible, we face the natural high level of stress to find the right job at the right pay in the right part of the country. How do we stay emotionally healthy in that environment? According to the verse above, we are to cast our cares upon the Lord, and he will sustain us.

By casting our cares upon God and then believing that he will sustain us while we look for work, we can find relief from the stress, because he is faithful to his people and to his Word. Notice, however, that God's promise to sustain us is conditional. We cast, then he sustains.

DIGGING DEEPER INTO PSALM 55:22

1. When was the last time you lost a job?

2. Describe the stress you felt to find a new position.

3. Do a quick inventory of all your possessions. How much money do you spend in an average month on entertainment? How much do you save each month for "a rainy day"?

4. If you spend too much, list two things you can do to change that.

5. What do you think "casting your cares" upon God means? How successful have you been at doing so during difficult financial times?

28

No More Grudges

> And when you stand praying, if you hold anything against anyone, forgive him, so that your Father in heaven may forgive you your sins.
>
> Mark 11:25

Have you ever had a friend betray your confidence? Friendships often end after such an event, and unless the betrayal is properly dealt with, grudges set in and cause bitterness toward the other person—sometimes to the point of lashing out at him or her. The person returns the fire, and it turns into an all-out war.

Grudges start with the belief that we have the right to hold ill feelings toward someone because of a wrong done against us. Grudges make us feel self-righteous and powerful. Yet they do far more harm to us than to the one toward whom they are directed, and that defeats the purpose of holding a grudge, doesn't it? And let's be honest; we hold grudges because we want to get back at the other person for the pain that person caused us. The last thing we want to do is forgive somebody because it means giving up the "right" to get even.

The desire to get back at someone after he or she has harmed us is normal. We are human, and emotions can get the best of us. But in the above verse, God calls the Christian to a higher standard. First, Jesus assumes that Christians will converse with God. Then he makes a point that ought to stop us from ever holding grudges: If we hold anything against *anyone*, we are to forgive him or her so that God will forgive our sins.

Forgiveness has little to do with letting someone off the hook. Instead, it frees our hearts and emotions. More importantly, it puts us in a position to be forgiven for our own sins. All of us have wronged other people—either intentionally or accidentally. We can't receive forgiveness for those sins unless we are willing to forgive others for the wrong they've done to us.

DIGGING DEEPER INTO MARK 11:25

1. Are you currently holding a grudge against somebody? If so, name the person.

2. What specifically did he or she do to you?

3. Have you become bitter as a result of holding the grudge?

4. How has holding on to a grudge affected your spiritual health?

5. What should you do in order to forgive the person who wronged you?

29

From a Curse to a Blessing

> For they [Ammonites and Moabites] did not come to meet you with bread and water on your way when you came out of Egypt, and they hired Balaam ... to pronounce a curse on you. However, the LORD your God would not listen to Balaam but turned the curse into a blessing for you, because the LORD your God loves you.
>
> Deuteronomy 23:4–5

In 1981 Stan's wife informed him that she wanted a separation. He got into his car, drove to a store, purchased a rope, and intended to hang himself. He wasn't a Christian at the time, and he didn't think he could handle the emotional pain. God intervened, but his wife divorced him soon thereafter.

After struggling with his emotional health for eighteen years, Stan became a Christian in 1999. He had recently retired, so he spent a lot of time in the Scriptures, under the wing of his new pastor. It was time well spent, and Stan developed a good understanding about how to handle his struggles with emotional pain.

"The primary thing that I have been doing when feelings of loneliness and despair come over me is to, first of all, go to the Lord in prayer and thanksgiving, and then stop feeling sorry for myself and get up and start doing something," Stan said. He reads his Bible or a Christian book, he takes walks, and he finds ways to serve in his church. "My old methods were to just sit around and brood and feel sorry for myself. I have found by concentrating on the Lord and all the blessings that he gives me every day, my sadness is being relieved."

In the above verses, Balaam pronounced a curse on God's people with the intention of harming them, but God turned their curse into a blessing because he loved his people. In a sense, God is doing the same thing for Stan. God is taking the pain of Stan's divorce and showing him how much he loves him by helping him concentrate on everything God has done for him.

Stan's struggle to feel emotionally healthy since his divorce has not been easy. But by seeing God involved in his everyday affairs, he feels as if he is on the road to recovery.

DIGGING DEEPER INTO DEUTERONOMY 23:4-5

1. Have you ever felt so blue that you had thoughts of hurting yourself? (If you have those types of thoughts now—*run* to your pastor or some other trusted person for help! God can restore you and ease your pain.)

2. If you struggle with feeling blue, describe your battle.

3. How often do you think about God's love for you when you feel blue?

4. List three positive actions you can take the next time you feel down.

5. List everything that you can think of for which you are thankful to God.

30

A Higher Standard

> These commandments that I give you today are to be upon your hearts. Impress them on your children. Talk about them when you sit at home and when you walk along the road, when you lie down and when you get up.
>
> Deuteronomy 6:6–7

Ted grew up in a family environment that far too many children today experience—a substance abuse home. His father drank too much, which led to fights between his mother and father. They didn't fight in front of Ted or his siblings, but the kids could sometimes hear the shouting from their upstairs bedroom.

"My father wasn't normally a violent man when he drank," Ted told me. "But one night my mom must have thought he was about to cross the line, because she ran into our bedroom and locked the door after one of their fights." His dad left the house that night—symbolic of the way he'd emotionally left his family years earlier. Ted's parents divorced shortly thereafter, and his father remarried.

Ted was like every other boy. He loved his father and wanted to spend time with him. On Saturdays they spent time in the park, went to carnivals, ate meals out, and oddly, played pinball in neighborhood bars. Ted's father drank while they were there, but Ted didn't care because he was spending time with his father.

One Saturday, after a day of pinball at the bar, Ted went to his father's apartment, where his father and his father's new wife got into a shouting match about alcohol. "I remember that day so clearly," Ted said. "I made a decision that day. I was twelve years old, and I promised myself I would never treat my future wife or children the way my father had." That promise helped him cope with his father's drunkenness.

After Ted became a Christian, the verses from Deuteronomy 6 gave him a clear vision for his future if God one day chooses to bless him with a wife and children. Ted intends to raise the standard of living from the depths of the substance abuse home of his past to one that speaks of God's commands every day.

DIGGING DEEPER INTO DEUTERONOMY 6:6–7

1. Have you or somebody you know grown up in a substance abuse environment?

2. Describe the environment that you or your friend grew up in. Were one or both parents violent? Were they negligent?

3. How openly did your family (or your friend's family) discuss the substance abuse problem?

4. How did you (or your friend) cope with that poor family life environment?

5. How could Ted's example of focusing on these verses help you (or your friend) become empowered so that you do not repeat the cycle of substance abuse in your family?

Part 4

Physical Desires

All singles struggle with physical desires. Maybe some struggle less than others, but nonetheless, the struggle exists. God built physical desires into our bodies, and he considers them good. He also designed the marriage bed to express and live out those physical desires. Any other way of meeting those desires cheapens the marriage bed and our bodies.

What, then, does God tell single people to do with their physical desires? What should we do about impure thoughts that come into our minds? What do we do when we burn with desire? And what if we never marry? Are we supposed to keep our physical desires in check our entire lives? Tough questions to answer.

No matter where we are in our struggle to remain pure, all of us have a common enemy: sexual fantasies. Sexual sin begins with fantasies. In this section of the book, we will explore specific biblical methods to cleanse our minds so we can stay pure. We need to take sexual fantasies seriously because they are never satisfied to stay in our minds. They want more. They demand more. They progressively march toward some form of fornication until they are satisfied.

Beyond the damage that sexual sins cause to our bodies and our souls, they also bring harm to the object of our lust—even if we've never touched the other person. Harboring sexual fantasies about someone degrades him or her and makes the arrogant and sinful assumption that God created that person to fulfill our physical desires. So we'll also spend some time looking at the damage our physical desires can cause other people when these drives aren't handled properly.

Staying pure in thought and deed isn't easy. But the Bible doesn't gloss over this area of our lives. In fact, it speaks directly to it.

For the next ten days, let's open our hearts to hearing from God about how we can control our physical desires and rely on God to provide the strength necessary to do it.

31

Out with the Old, In with the New

> You were taught, with regard to your former way of life, to put off your old self, which is being corrupted by its deceitful desires; to be made new in the attitude of your minds; and to put on the new self, created to be like God in true righteousness and holiness.
>
> Ephesians 4:22–24

Often I end up in tears over this struggle." Nancy is in a relationship with a man who is better able than she to resist the temptation to give in to physical desires. She feels guilty for wanting to fulfill her desires, and she doesn't know what to do.

In the above verses, the apostle Paul told us to put off our old self and put on the new by letting who we are in Christ, not our "deceitful desires," drive us. How do we do that? The answer is contained in the remainder of the verse. Our new self was created to be like God in true righteousness and holiness. Just as our old self was controlled by our sin nature, our new self was created to be controlled by God.

It starts with a steady diet of Scripture. As we implement what we have learned, the new self takes control. As this becomes our standard practice, physical desires have less appeal. The old self will never truly stop fighting with us until we enter glory, but it won't be able to punch hard enough to knock us down if we are more concerned with pleasing God than fulfilling our desires.

Don't worry about trying to muster up the strength to fight against your physical desires way into the future. You'll feel defeated before you ever get started because you know you don't have the power to control them forever. You'll think about your failures before they even happen. Give up your physical desires to God, and he will provide the power in his grace to overcome them as you begin your fight today.

1. Have you ever felt like Nancy did?

2. What were you doing at the time to try to overcome your physical desires?

3. How does your way of overcoming your physical desires compare or contrast with the way Paul suggested?

4. What does it mean to put on your new self?

5. Write a prayer to God committing to put on your new self today.

32

Longing Eyes, Running Legs

She caught him by his cloak and said, "Come to bed with me!" But he left his cloak in her hand and ran out of the house.

Genesis 39:12

Joseph was twenty-eight years old when Potiphar's wife propositioned him (see Gen. 41:1, 46). He was a single man who had been unjustly sold into slavery at the age of seventeen by his brothers, but God was with him as he served Potiphar faithfully for eleven years.

Joseph didn't have a wife. As far as we know, he was still a virgin at the age of twenty-eight. He certainly had all the same physical desires you and I have. A proposition from Potiphar's wife must have appealed to his flesh.

In spite of his physical desires, however, he spoke directly to her and asked how he could do such a wicked thing against God (Gen. 39:9). His rebuke didn't stop her. Genesis 39:10 says, "And though she spoke to Joseph day after day, he refused to go to bed with her or even be with her." Not only did he have to fight off temptation once, he had to do it repeatedly.

When she finally caught him alone one day and tried to seduce him by physically grabbing his cloak, he ran out of the house, leaving his cloak in her hand. You know the rest of the story. He was imprisoned because Potiphar's shunned wife accused Joseph of attempting to sleep with her.

How did Joseph stay so strong in the midst of continual temptation? Look at the last few words of verse 10: "or even be with her." He didn't put himself in a position to fall. At first he avoided her. Eventually he ran—probably because it was getting more difficult to say no.

His three-step approach of refusal, avoidance, and fleeing kept him from falling into sin and from losing the blessings of God on his life (see Gen. 45:8).

1. Have you ever received a direct invitation to bed from a member of the opposite sex? Explain.

2. Joseph is thought to have been twenty-eight when Potiphar's wife propositioned him. How justified do you feel about giving in to sexual temptation as you get older?

3. How does Joseph's refusal, avoidance, and fleeing the situation compare or contrast to the way you've handled advances in the past?

4. How has this passage empowered you to handle a direct request for sexual activity outside of marriage?

5. If Joseph had given in, he would have lost God's blessing (Gen. 45:8). What are some of the ramifications of giving in to sexual temptation?

33

First Kisses, No Second Guesses

> The wife's body does not belong to her alone but also to her husband. In the same way, the husband's body does not belong to him alone but also to his wife.
>
> 1 Corinthians 7:4

When Adrian Burwell and Jill Merry got married recently, they shared their first kiss in front of more than six hundred people who attended their wedding. "To me, the first kiss is one of the most precious gifts I can give away, and it's something I'll only give my wife," Burwell said.

Merry felt the same way. "I knew I didn't want to date around and give different parts of my heart to different guys. I just decided I wanted to save my first kiss for my wedding day," she said.[3]

How did they restrain themselves? They set guidelines early in the relationship and stuck to them. They had normal physical desires like everyone does, but they were both thinking about staying pure for their future spouse's sake. Their motivation was grounded in Scripture.

In 1 Corinthians 7:4, Paul made a statement that sounds foreign to our culture: Our bodies do not belong to us. They belong to Christ (1 Cor. 6:19) and to our future spouses if God intends for us to marry. And if he intends us for marriage, then a day is coming when we'll have to tell our future spouses about our sexual history. They do have a right to know whether we were saving ourselves for them or not.

What does that mean for those who haven't saved themselves? Is it too late for them? Let's flip the situation around and see if we can answer that question. Imagine that it's time for the discussion about sexual history between you and your future spouse. Your future spouse confesses sexual sin but is quick to tell you that he or she repented after realizing that his or her body belonged to God and you. How would you respond to such humility?

Whether you have been sexually pure in the past or not, you have a responsibility not only to God but to your potential future spouse to stay pure from this moment on. He or she has a right to expect purity from you.

DIGGING DEEPER INTO 1 CORINTHIANS 7:4

1. What was the first thought that ran through your mind when you read about Adrian and Jill's first kiss happening on the altar?

2. Do you agree with where they drew the line? If so, why? If not, where would you draw the line and why?

3. Pretend that you are meeting with a potential spouse and that he or she has just asked you about your sexual history. What would you say?

4. During that same conversation, your potential spouse tells you that he or she has been sexually active in the past but has since repented with his or her future spouse in mind. How would you respond?

5. If you need to repent from sexual sin, write down your prayer of repentance.

34

Quick! Where's the Escape Hatch?

> No temptation has seized you except what is common to man. And God is faithful; he will not let you be tempted beyond what you can bear. But when you are tempted, he will also provide a way out so that you can stand up under it.
>
> 1 Corinthians 10:13

John is a thirty-eight-year-old who struggles with physical desires. Not long ago he went on a church singles retreat during which the group took a tour of the downtown area of the large city they were visiting. During the tour, several provocatively dressed women walked by and caught John's eye.

Knowing he was surrounded by people from his church helped him turn his head away before he began to lust for the women he'd seen. In this particular instance, the "way of escape" that God provided when John was tempted was John's consciousness of the fact that he was with people from church. He didn't want to lust in front of them.

If you struggle with physical desires, you may feel as if your sex drive is abnormal and that something is wrong with you. Chances are that you are a normal human being with a healthy sex drive. Look back at verse 13 again. "No temptation has seized you except what is common to man." The temptation you are experiencing is common to everyone. So don't let your struggles isolate you from the body of Christ, but rather depend on fellow believers to help you through your struggles.

John either meets or speaks on the phone with a man from church once a week to help build him up in Christ and keep him accountable. It's not a relationship of judgment when John fails but rather one that lovingly helps keep him on track and better prepared for the next instance when he will be tempted.

The combination of God always providing a way of escape and John surrounding himself with Christians who love him helps him battle his temptation to give in to physical desire.

DIGGING DEEPER INTO 1 CORINTHIANS 10:13

1. If you have a wandering eye, what are your strategies to keep it under control?

2. What have you thought about 1 Corinthians 10:13 in the past?

3. How has God made a way of escape for you in the past as he did for John?

4. Normally, how willing are you to look for God's way of escape?

5. Name one or two friends who could be built-in escape hatches for you like John's friends.

35

The Power to Endure

> Therefore, get rid of all moral filth and the evil that is so prevalent and humbly accept the word planted in you, which can save you.
>
> Do not merely listen to the word, and so deceive yourselves. Do what it says.
>
> James 1:21–22

Before I became a Christian, I listened to a style of music called "crotch rock," which was aptly named because the lyrics spoke so much about fornication. Of course, the songwriters didn't call it "fornication." They called it sex and several other words I won't repeat. But by failing to accept God's parameters for sexual relations, they corrupted the wonder and beauty of sex, as God intended, into moral filth.

After my conversion to Christ, I tossed more than a thousand dollars' worth of compact discs into the junkyard. Most of the music I threw away fit into the "crotch rock" genre, so it belonged in the junkyard. Some of the music I tossed didn't fall into that genre, but I was too young in the faith to discern what I should keep, so I tossed it all. It was my way of getting rid of moral filth.

Moral filth wraps itself in a glittery package and pretends to solve our problems, but in reality, moral filth entices our sinful nature. As Christian singles, some of us toy with sexual fantasies, some of us view pornography, and some of us go way too far physically with a boyfriend or girlfriend. In all three cases, we may try to justify our actions by saying sexual relations are normal, so we can't stop. James would disagree. Ridding ourselves of moral filth puts us in a position to receive God's empowerment to endure temptation if we obey the remainder of the verse.

After we've rid ourselves of moral filth, James tells us to "humbly accept the word planted in you." Humbly accepting something means to accept it without the slightest hint of arrogance or pride. We just accept it as truth, knowing and trusting that it has the power to change us.

Next he tells us to "not merely listen to the word" but also "do what it says." That sounds simple enough, but obedience always comes with a cost. In my case, it was over a thousand dollars in CDs. In yours, it could be the loss of a boyfriend or girlfriend who doesn't want to stop going too far physically. Whatever you may lose, consider the cost of your loss in light of the freedom you will gain to endure temptation and live as God designed you to live.

DIGGING DEEPER INTO JAMES 1:21–22

1. How does lust usually wrap itself up in a glittery package in your experience?

2. When you read a Scripture verse that challenges your sexual conduct, how quick are you to change?

3. If your response to Scripture verses that challenge your sexual conduct is not immediate, how do you normally justify a delayed response?

4. If you have any sexual moral filth in your life right now, what steps will you take to get rid of it?

5. Commit to spending more time in God's Word, approaching it with a humble heart, seeking correction.

36

Starving the Flesh Dog

> Those who live according to the sinful nature have their minds set on what that nature desires; but those who live in accordance with the Spirit have their minds set on what the Spirit desires. The mind of sinful man is death, but the mind controlled by the Spirit is life and peace.
>
> Romans 8:5–6

The Christian media used to ask former University of Nebraska football receivers coach Ron Brown how he avoided giving in to the lust for power. Such a desire is natural for many assistant coaches who aspire to become head coaches regardless of whether God wants them to move up or not. In response to media questions, Coach Brown gave this example.

Everybody has two dogs—a flesh dog and a spirit dog. Both are competing for control. Only one can win. The dog that wins guides his owner. Although it sounds as if the person watching the fight is passive, he is actually in control. He's the one who feeds the dogs. If he feeds the flesh dog, the flesh dog wins. If he feeds the spirit dog, the spirit dog wins. If he feeds both dogs, it leads to a long drawn-out battle that neither dog wins without a bloody fight.

The same principle applies to our physical desires. When we choose to feed our flesh with inappropriate movies or Internet sites and lingering looks at members of the opposite sex, our physical desires demand to be met. When we choose to feed our spirit with the Scriptures, prayer, good Internet sites, and good movies, then our spirit is enriched, and we are enabled to walk in holiness.

Coach Brown's illustration has helped me better understand Paul's words in Romans 8:5–6. We can choose which nature to feed—our natural sinful nature or our new nature in Christ. When I struggle with physical desires now, I go back and determine which dog I've been feeding. Almost every time I've done this, I can point to a specific instance where I've fed the flesh instead of or more than the Spirit. That's when I know it is time to starve the flesh dog.

DIGGING DEEPER INTO ROMANS 8:5–6

1. On a scale of 1 to 10, with 1 being totally helpless, how would you rate your battle to control your physical desires?

2. In the past, how have you been active in feeding the spirit and starving your flesh when you were struggling with physical desires?

3. List all of the movies, CDs, and television programs you've watched or listened to in the past seven days.

4. Have these fed your spirit, your flesh, or both? Explain.

5. If your answer was your flesh or both, what five things can you do in the next week to feed your spirit instead? Share these with a friend and ask your friend to keep you accountable.

37

The Ripple Effect of Sexual Impurity

> It is God's will that you should be sanctified: that you should avoid sexual immorality; that each of you should learn to control his own body in a way that is holy and honorable, not in passionate lust like the heathen, who do not know God; and that in this matter no one should wrong his brother or take advantage of him.
>
> 1 Thessalonians 4:3–6

In the above verses, Paul tells us we should learn to control our bodies in a way that is holy and honorable. Notice the phrase "learn to control." Sanctification is a process. This side of heaven, we will never reach perfection. In fact, those who expect or think that sanctification is instant will be disappointed and perhaps will give in to temptation after losing a few battles. Instead, sanctification always moves forward—sometimes even after a fall and quick repentance. The falls are never acceptable in God's sight, but quick repentance puts us back on the path of sanctification.

One way to minimize our falls is to consider verse 6: "That in this matter no one should wrong his brother or take advantage of him." At first glance, these words seem out of place given their context, but of course, they are exactly where God wants them. Sexual sin never affects only the one who sins. It takes advantage of the weaknesses in the other party. Even if the sin is untamed lust, when we give in to it, we degrade the person we lust after by thinking about him or her as simply an object for our pleasure.

We need to think of people in their entirety. Nearly everybody has an extended family or friends who love him or her. Everybody has emotions. Everybody has a soul. Let's reject the lie that our sexual sin doesn't hurt anyone but ourselves. And in so doing we learn to control our bodies by never forgetting that the object of our desires is not an object but a living, breathing human being whom God created to bring himself glory.

DIGGING DEEPER INTO 1 THESSALONIANS 4:3–6

1. How often do you feel like giving up the fight because you continue to struggle with your physical desires?

2. How quickly do you normally repent of lust?

3. When you struggle with lust, how often do you think about the entirety of the person you are lusting after?

4. How have these verses from 1 Thessalonians changed or solidified your belief that sexual sin always affects those beyond yourself?

5. How can viewing the people you lust after as complete people—with families, emotions, and souls—motivate you to learn to control your body?

38

A Covenant with My Eyes

> I made a covenant with my eyes
> not to look lustfully at a girl.
>
> Job 31:1

Just before summer began a couple of years ago, John, a single friend of mine from church, sent me an email. It simply said, "I'm praying for God to protect our eyes during the upcoming summer months, since some women will be dressed inappropriately."

I imagine that I'm no different than most men—Christian or not. I don't need any help spotting attractive females. Throw in the fact that our culture applauds women who dress provocatively with the sole purpose of getting people to notice their bodies, and a struggle with lustful thoughts ensues.

That's why I appreciated John's email so much. Not only did he understand and admit that we need God's help in protecting our eyes, but he went a step further and prayed for God's protection of our eyes. John's email reminded me of Job's comment in the above verse.

Job (like John) made his decision *before* an attractive woman passed in front of his eyes. He didn't wait until a woman crossed his path and then try to turn away. And look how serious Job took his covenant. In Job 31:9–10, he said, "If my heart has been enticed by a woman, or if I have lurked at my neighbor's door, then may my wife grind another man's grain, and may other men sleep with her."

Job made a covenant with his eyes because he knew that if he allowed his eyes to lust, his heart would follow. So he didn't let it get that far. How many of us would be willing to make the vow Job made in verses 9 and 10 toward our potential future spouse? I don't think God calls us to make such a vow, but imagine how serious we would be about protecting our eyes and ultimately our hearts if we did. Even if God doesn't call us to make such a vow, he does call us to moral purity. Making a covenant with our eyes not to look lustfully upon a member of the opposite sex would be a great way to start.

DIGGING DEEPER INTO JOB 31:1

1. Describe your personal struggle with looking lustfully at members of the opposite sex.

2. What have you tried to do to avoid looking lustfully at members of the opposite sex?

3. How successful have your methods been?

4. If you are willing to make a covenant with your eyes right now not to look lustfully at members of the opposite sex, write the covenant down here.

5. Job was bold enough to tell his friends about the covenant he made with his eyes. Are you willing to do the same thing? If so, write down the name(s) of the person(s) you are going to tell, and follow through today.

39

For God's Glory

> So whether you eat or drink or whatever you do, do it all for the glory of God. Do not cause anyone to stumble, whether Jews, Greeks or the church of God.
>
> 1 Corinthians 10:31–32

By the age of nineteen, Amy had been a Christian for six years, but she wasn't discipled, and that led to a struggle with sexual sin. "I tried to draw a line between sexual impurity and fornication, which does not exist," she said. "Having justified my behavior, I continued until one day I crossed the line and committed the act of fornication."

At the time she had a boyfriend who showed some interest in the faith, but she doesn't think he was a Christian. "By my allowing this physical behavior to continue, I was inadvertently reinforcing the behavior and allowing him to believe that it is okay with God," she said. "In actuality I should have set the standard and explained to him why my life should be pleasing to God. As a result, it might have made him redefine his relationship with Christ."

In the verse above, the apostle Paul tells us that everything we do is to bring glory to God. However, he doesn't stop there. He also tells us that our actions should not cause someone else to stumble. The two go hand in hand. When we do things that bring God glory, we reflect God's character to those who are watching. When we do things that are not God-honoring, we cause those around us to stumble.

When Amy realized that she had caused her boyfriend to stumble, she was so upset that she decided to make a change. She became more active in church and formed strong relationships there. She also received the training that she desperately needed to live the Christian life. During that period of time, her focus turned from her needs to the needs of others, which in turn became the key for her in dealing with physical desires.

"As time progressed, and I was renewing my mind with the Word of God, the urges seemed to have died down," she said. "As of today, I just need a hug."

DIGGING DEEPER INTO 1 CORINTHIANS 10:31-32

1. Amy tried to draw lines between certain intimate activities and fornication. Where do you draw the line?

2. Have you based the line upon what you thought was right or upon what you saw in Scripture? Explain.

3. How have you justified your actions in the past by thinking that since you had not crossed the line you drew, you were not fornicating?

4. What one step can you take this week to better handle your physical desires?

5. How would your life be different if you decided to handle your physical desires to the glory of God?

40

Our Spiritual Act of Worship

> Therefore, I urge you, brothers, in view of God's mercy,
> to offer your bodies as living sacrifices, holy and pleasing
> to God—this is your spiritual act of worship.
>
> Romans 12:1

God's long-term answer for most people regarding the satisfaction of their sexual desires is marriage. But what are singles supposed to do in the present? And what about the future for those of us whom God calls to lifelong singleness?

Singles of all ages and stages of life have the same physical desires as everyone else, and somehow it seems unfair to us that the only God-given way to satisfy those desires is in a covenantal marriage relationship that he hasn't given us yet or may never give us.

The apostle Paul offers an answer in Romans 12:1 that makes most of us cringe—sacrifice. It's a concept we don't like because it means we have to give something up, but that's only part of the story. Sacrifice always includes another element—love. Sometimes we make sacrifices for people we love. Sometimes we make sacrifices for people we don't know, but we do it because we love God and we know it pleases him.

When you sacrifice your time, money, or talents to help someone, do you fret over how much you had to sacrifice in order to help that person, or do you find great satisfaction and added meaning in your life knowing that your sacrifice helped someone in need? Sacrifice brings joy and contentment, doesn't it?

Why then do we as singles dwell on what we're missing? God's people have no rights over their bodies. We have no right to demand that our physical desires get met. God is happy to do so within the context of marriage, and someday he may choose to give us a spouse. But until then we can show our love for him by laying our physical desires on the sacrificial altar as an act of worship. And in so doing, we will experience the joy and contentment that always come from sacrifice.

DIGGING DEEPER INTO ROMANS 12:1

1. If another single person of the same gender asked you what he or she was supposed to do with physical desires while waiting for a spouse, how would you respond?

2. When somebody tells you that you are supposed to sacrifice something, what is the first thing that comes into your mind?

3. Have you ever thought about the element of love in the concept of sacrifice? Explain.

4. How can you offer your physical desires as an act of worship to God?

5. If you have never done so, write a prayer offering God your physical desires today as an act of worship.

Part 5

Longing for Love

Romantic comedies and inspirational romance novels never go out of season because so many of us long for love—including married people whose spouses cannot compare with the romantic leading men or beautiful women they see on-screen. Watching or reading about two people falling in love after overcoming impossible odds gives us hope, even if we are momentarily discouraged with our current circumstances.

As Christians, we serve the God of impossibility. He can bring two people together any time he wants to, regardless of how many obstacles lie in their paths. Shouldn't our hope of finding a spouse come from knowing this about God rather than from what a writer puts in print or on the big screen?

We search for a perfect match, but only God can provide one. We long to tell him or her our thoughts, dreams, and fears. We long for the emotional security that comes from a person knowing every detail about our lives and still accepting us as we are. We long to know that person better than we know ourselves. We long for the physical closeness only a spouse can or should bring.

In our longing for love, we can miss God's plan for our lives right now. Our longing can drive us to focus so much on our possible future that we believe our current season in life is a waste of time. When that attitude sets in, we are unmotivated to serve God with our whole heart during our season of singleness. Longing for love isn't wrong until it reaches the point of eclipsing what God wants to do with us today.

The Bible calls us to live out our purpose as singles in obedience to God's call on our lives and to persevere until God either brings us a spouse or calls us home. For the next ten days, we will study what God has to say about perseverance and obedience as you seek to keep your longing for love in perspective.

41

God's Road

> Therefore, since we are surrounded by such a great cloud
> of witnesses, let us throw off everything that hinders and
> the sin that so easily entangles, and let us run with per-
> severance the race marked out for us.
>
> Hebrews 12:1

Western Christians often view themselves as *individu-
als* living out their lives for Christ. The Scriptures
paint a different picture. The verse above refers to a great
cloud of witnesses surrounding us as believers. The writer
of Hebrews refers to the saints who have gone before us
(see Hebrews 11). In a sense, those who have persevered
through tremendous hardship, and even martyrdom, for
the sake of the kingdom are watching and encouraging the
church here on earth to do the same.

As we long for love, we need to keep in mind that God
has a plan for his church. He intends for some in his church
to marry. He intends for some in his church to remain single.
Either way, he calls his church to persevere together as we
pursue our individual purposes and the tasks he has given
each of us to do. We are to run the race he has put in front
of us with his kingdom in mind. As we each pursue the
plans God has for us, his overall purpose is furthered.

As we run the race, we'll discover many additional roads
along the way that could take us far from the finish line God
intended. "Marriage Road" may be one of those. Perhaps
God intends you to take Marriage Road, but he hasn't placed
it in your path for several years. Don't veer off the road he
has put in front of you in search of Marriage Road. He'll
point you in another direction when he is ready.

To persevere on the road that God has marked out for you, set a good steady jogging pace and throw off anything that would try to get you to change courses. Don't slow down to examine roads you shouldn't go down. Don't speed up to see if Marriage Road is just around the corner. Set a pace, stay on the road, and make your mark for God's kingdom.

DIGGING DEEPER INTO HEBREWS 12:1

1. How often do you think about the hardships that the saints of old endured?

2. Read Hebrews 11:30–40. How does your hardship of longing for love compare with what these saints endured?

3. How does knowing this make it easier to accept the road that God has marked out for you—even if he never intends for you to marry?

4. How often do you stop to examine roads that you know you shouldn't pursue? What can you do to speed up your pace instead?

5. How often do you sprint ahead of God to find out if Marriage Road is right around the corner? What can you do to slow down your pace?

42

Eyes for Another God

If you love me, you will obey what I command.

John 14:15

Longing for love is an integral part of being human. We all experience it, yet some singles tend to give this normal longing too high of a priority. We get so caught up in trying to appease this need that we neglect the duties God has given us.

The simple statement Jesus made in John 14:15 is a good test of whether you are giving your need for love too high of a priority. Jesus turns the table on us and wants to know if we love *him* more than anything else. He's much more interested in our actions than our words because our actions reveal our hearts.

Have you ever been in a relationship with someone you suspected didn't love you as much as you loved him or her? What fueled your suspicion? Actions, right? Maybe he or she wasn't as enthusiastic as you expected or didn't express an interest in taking the relationship to the next level. Whatever the case, his or her actions led you to conclude that the love wasn't genuine.

Jesus made the same conclusion. Actions matter, and when we fail to do what the Scriptures command, or when we disobey promptings of the Holy Spirit because we are more concerned with our desire to find a spouse, our actions reveal an unfaithful heart to Christ. We have a wandering eye for another god.

If you have noticed that you have more interest in feeding your longing for love than in obeying Christ, it's not too late to change. Repent of your sin and then wait in anticipation for God's gentle whisper the next time you have a decision to make. Show Jesus that you love him more than anyone or anything else.

1. List at least one scriptural command that you are failing to obey right now.

2. Write down one or more promptings you've received lately from the Holy Spirit that you have failed to obey.

3. What was your justification for disobedience in both cases?

4. How has your longing for love interfered with your relationship with Christ?

5. If you need to repent for disobedience or for placing too high of a priority on finding love, write your prayer of repentance here.

43

The Bigger Picture

> Return home, my daughters; I am too old to have another husband. Even if I thought there was still hope for me—even if I had a husband tonight and then gave birth to sons—would you wait until they grew up?
>
> Ruth 1:12–13

Naomi's two sons married women whom she grew to love. After her sons died, as painful as it was, she wanted her daughters-in-law to return to their families, hoping they would find new husbands. In trying to convince them to go, Naomi revealed that she still longed for love after the death of her own husband, who died shortly before her sons did. Look at her words in the above verse: "Even if I thought there was still hope for me . . ." She did her best to hide her feelings, but she couldn't.

She didn't want her daughters-in-law to worry about her. In fact, she even helped one of them, Ruth, find a new husband. Against Naomi's wishes, instead of returning to her home, Ruth traveled back to Bethlehem with her. In the third chapter of Ruth, after Naomi discovered that Ruth had been to Boaz's threshing floor, she pushed Ruth to wash up, put on perfume, and dress in her best clothes for a return visit, knowing that Boaz was a kinsman-redeemer in their family.

Ruth eventually married Boaz, and they bore a child named Obed. Obed became the father of Jesse, who became the father of David, whose line generations later produced the Messiah. Naomi had no way of knowing that her efforts to help Ruth would eventually lead to such a world-changing event, but it did. She was part of a bigger plan.

Like Naomi, we may never know the long-term results of our service to God today, and we may never see the bigger picture of God's purpose, but by persevering through our own longings, God may use us as his change agent for tomorrow and generations to come.

1. Naomi longed for love, but she also had other priorities in her life that required her attention. To what extent do you identify with her?

2. What has God put on your heart right now that you need to do?

3. If you had been in Naomi's place, what would you have done?

4. What friend or relative in your life could you encourage to seek God's will in some matter?

5. Think of one way God could use you to change the world, as he did with Naomi.

44

Delight Yourself in the Lord

> Delight yourself in the LORD
> and he will give you the desires of your heart.
>
> Psalm 37:4

I gave birth to my son at the age of seventeen," Cindy recently told me. "Holding him in my arms, I wept. 'It's just you and me,' I told him, caressing his tiny head. His father abandoned us four months before this miracle entered the world. My hunger to be loved overwhelmed me."

Have you ever felt like Cindy? I have. In the midst of my turmoil, I've often turned to Psalm 37:4 and meditated on it. I love the idea of God giving me the desires of my heart, but that promise has a condition—delight myself in the Lord. That's the hard part of the verse—the place where I have to ask myself whether I am truly delighting myself in the Lord.

One day I wondered how the Bible defined "delighting" myself in the Lord. I knew it wasn't an abstract concept. Two verses that I found helped me to know if I was really delighting myself in the Lord or not:

Psalm 40:8—"I delight to do Your will, O my God, and Your law is within my heart" (NKJV).

Romans 7:22—For in my inner being I delight in God's law.

How do we delight ourselves in the Lord? By doing what pleases him and putting his law in our hearts. Then, as we are sanctified, he gives us the desires of our heart. Here's how Matthew Henry put it: "He has not promised to gratify all the appetites of the body and the humours of the fancy, but to grant all the desires of the heart, all the cravings of the renewed sanctified soul. What is the desire of the heart of a good man? It is this, to know, and love, and live to God, to please him and to be pleased in him."[4]

Imagine what our desires would be and how God would meet them if we spent more time on the first part of Psalm 37:4 than the last part.

DIGGING DEEPER INTO PSALM 37:4

1. How have you dealt with your longing for love?

2. Describe your thoughts when reading Psalm 37:4 in the past.

3. After looking at two other Scripture verses about delighting ourselves in the Lord, and after reading Matthew Henry's quote, how have these helped you better understand Psalm 37:4?

4. What can you do to delight yourself in the Lord?

5. How do you think your desires will be different if you do the things you listed in the previous question?

45

What Drives Your Longing?

A longing fulfilled is sweet to the soul,
but fools detest turning from evil.

Proverbs 13:19

Many things can satisfy your flesh, but only what is God-ordained can satisfy your soul. Often when we long for love, we consider only the benefits that a spouse could bring to our lives. We rarely think about how our fulfilled longing could be sweet to our souls, as Proverbs says. As natural as our longing for love is, it is often self-focused. It cannot satisfy the soul until we forget about the benefits of marriage and think more about what we can bring to a marriage.

How does a "fool who detests turning from evil" fit into this equation? Matthew Henry answers the question this way: "There are in man strong desires of happiness; God has provided for the accomplishment of those desires, and that would be sweet to the soul, whereas the pleasures of sense are grateful only to the carnal appetite." He goes on to say, "Yet they will not be happy; for it is an abomination to them to depart from evil, which is necessary to their being happy."[5]

The evil Henry refers to is the focus we put on ourselves during our longings. We long for a spouse because we want someone to know us intimately. We long for a spouse because we don't want to spend Saturday nights alone. We long for a spouse because we have physical desires. That's not to say that God automatically grants a spouse to anyone willing to love sacrificially. But those who love others—friends, relatives, or neighbors—with a sacrificial heart have their souls fulfilled by God.

Putting both clauses of the verse above together, we can see that we can never have a fulfilled soul without turning from our own needs and longings, whether we're married or not. Our flesh might be fulfilled temporarily, but not our souls. Examine your longing for love and determine whether it is self-focused or others-focused. Your answer will give you a good idea about how Christlike you are becoming.

DIGGING DEEPER INTO PROVERBS 13:19

1. What drives your longing for love (loneliness, physical desires, something else)?

2. Is your previous answer more focused on your needs or the needs of others?

3. Have you ever thought about what you can bring to a marriage? List some things here.

4. How would those things serve your potential spouse?

5. Write down a prayer asking God to help you keep your mind fixed on him as you long for love. Also ask him to continually remind you to think about what you can bring to a marriage rather than what you will get out of it.

46

Civilian Affairs

> No one serving as a soldier gets involved in civilian affairs—he wants to please his commanding officer.
>
> 2 Timothy 2:4

Elisabeth Elliot tells the story about asking a man named Jim whom she went to college with to sign her yearbook. Jim had expressed an interest in her previously, but he was also convinced that he was to enter the mission field alone, because the area he was going to required singleness.

When Elisabeth peeked into her yearbook, she saw that Jim had signed his name in big sweeping letters, and underneath his signature he wrote, "2 Timothy 2:4." She ran to her dorm room to look the passage up. Imagine how she felt when she saw the above verse.

Even though Jim had feelings for Elisabeth, he wanted her to understand that his obedience to God was the top priority in his life, even if that meant they couldn't be together. God honored Jim's obedience, and after several years of waiting upon God, Jim Elliot married Elisabeth.

Soldiers don't have any say about whether they will go into war. When their company is called, they go, leaving spouses, children, and businesses behind. When soldiers enter the military, they surrender their right to act like civilians in exchange for a higher purpose. Likewise, as Christians, we don't have any say about whether we will do what God has called us to do. When he calls us, we are to go, leaving everything else behind if he so requires. We gave up our right to act like a civilian in exchange for God's higher purpose—the advancement of the gospel.

Our job is to obey God today; his job is everything else. We can be confident that if he intends for us to marry, he'll work out the details. If he doesn't intend us to marry, he'll satisfy our longing for love.

1. Describe the last time you thought you had met "the one," only to have circumstances pull you apart.

2. How did you see God at work in those circumstances?

3. In what ways are you like a soldier of Jesus—simply wanting to please your commanding officer?

4. In what ways are you unlike a soldier of Jesus—simply wanting to please your own longings?

5. How willing are you to trust God with your marital status?

47

Staying the Course

We rejoice and delight in you;
we will praise your love more than wine.

Song of Songs 1:4

The "beloved" in the Song of Songs was unafraid to admit her longing for her soon-to-be husband. In Song of Songs 3:1, she said, "All night long on my bed I looked for the one my heart loves; I looked for him but did not find him." She couldn't sleep because she couldn't stop thinking about the man she loved. Many scholars say that she was actually dreaming, and in her dream she felt compelled to find her future husband. Whether dream or reality, there is no mistaking how much she wanted to be close to him.

Listen to her words as she hunted for her future husband: "I held him and would not let him go till I had brought him to my mother's house, to the room of the one who conceived me" (Song of Songs 3:4). Her desires were so strong that she wanted to bring him to bed—an act that she didn't allow to happen at that point but wanted to. And her longing for love went beyond sexual desire. She longed to spend time with him, eating, and just enjoying his company (2:4–6).

So how did she persevere in her singleness while she longed for her future husband? She involved her friends in every aspect of her life—including her love life. Her friends spoke with her nine times in the book. They rejoiced and delighted with her in the verse above. They asked her tough questions about her beloved (Song of Songs 5:9). They offered to help her look for him when she couldn't find him (6:1).

In return, she was available to her friends, offering them advice about not awakening love before its time (Song of Songs 2:7). This group of friends kept each other on track. But they went beyond just asking tough questions; they had fun together too. They cared about each other's desires and were careful not to make light of them. By caring about each other the way they did, they never had to feel alone.

1. When was the last time you stayed awake at night because of your longing for love? Describe your emotions that night.

2. If you literally dream about finding the love of your life, describe one of your dreams.

3. Do your closest friends know how much you long for love? If not, why not?

4. How willing are you to give permission to your friends to ask you tough questions when you express an interest in a person?

5. How often do you help your friends through their longing for love by asking tough questions and listening with a nonjudgmental attitude?

48

Panting for God's Commands

> I open my mouth and pant,
>   longing for your commands.
>
> Psalm 119:131

Have you ever opened your mouth and panted for the commands of God? A few times in my life, I have. I was enraptured by God's Word and spent many hours in it. No matter what else was happening in my life at the time, I had an extreme sense of contentment. But I am always surprised by how easily I am pulled away from God and his commands when I long for something else.

The minute I long for something other than God and his commands, my sense of contentment and closeness to him is gone. Have you noticed a similar pattern in your own life? We can turn any desire, no matter how good, into an idol. As Christian singles in America today, I believe we are dangerously close to idolizing many things, including marriage.

When we notice that we've ceased to long for God's commands, that ought to get our attention. Our desire, or lack of desire, for God's commands is like a spiritual thermometer. It takes our spiritual temperature and reveals our heart's condition. A heart that doesn't pant with longing for God's commands has spiritual heart disease and is in desperate need of surgery—surgery that can be performed only by the Word of God.

Yet how can the Word of God fix the problem when we don't already long for God's commands? How will getting into the Word help us in our struggle with our longing for love? Dry periods come and go. Sometimes they are a result of unconfessed sin, and sometimes, quite honestly, they may simply be the result of our mood that day. Confess any known sin and then drink deeply of his Word. Psalm 119 is a great place to start. Pull out your Bible and read the entire psalm today. Let its spiritual nutrients cause you to pant for more and, in the process, help you to keep your longing for love in perspective.

Digging Deeper into Psalm 119:131

1. How often can you make the claim that the psalmist did in this verse?

2. Why don't you live like this more frequently?

3. What specific longing usually gets in the way of your longing for God?

4. Whose love do you long for more than anyone else's?

5. If your longing for love has become an idol, take some time to write a prayer of repentance below. If your longing for love is not an idol, what can you do to keep it from becoming one?

49

False Satisfaction

> For he satisfies the thirsty
> and fills the hungry with good things.
>
> Psalm 107:9

I have a confession to make. I love chick flicks. My male friends cringe every time a new romantic comedy hits the big screen because they know I'm going to drag them to see it. I think I lost all credibility with one friend when I talked him into seeing *Divine Secrets of the Ya-Ya Sisterhood*.

I've always loved these movies because I enjoy watching two people fall in love. Something is so natural and beautiful about that journey. But recently, while talking with a friend, I realized that my love for these movies is deeper than I knew. My friend asked me why these movies held such appeal for me. His question forced me to think about my love for these movies on a deeper level.

After pondering the question, I came to a realization. The movies that I enjoy the most portray characters with similar insecurities to mine and yet they are able to overcome and find somebody to love. Watching this happen satisfies my longing—albeit temporarily—for love. I experience their emotional turmoil as they struggle to make the relationship work, and I rejoice when it finally does.

Then I leave the theater feeling a little cheated. Not so much by the movie but by my own emotions. I've allowed my emotions to be engaged and satisfied for a moment. But the feeling quickly fades in the car ride home.

Examine Psalm 107:9. Why is satisfaction so temporary in instances like mine? Unless found solely in the Lord, satisfaction can't be anything but temporary. If I'm willing to sit through a two-hour chick flick for temporary satisfaction, how much more should I be willing and honored to spend time with God and his Word to find real satisfaction?

1. What activity brings temporary satisfaction to your longing for love?

2. How do you feel after the temporary satisfaction wears off?

3. Approximately how much time did you spend last month participating in the activity you listed in question 1?

4. For the upcoming month, commit to spending more time with God and his Word than you did last month with the activity that brings you a false sense of satisfaction.

5. Write down a realistic plan that you know you can stick to next month regarding how you will spend more time with God.

50

Let Nothing Move You

> Therefore, my dear brothers, stand firm. Let nothing
> move you. Always give yourselves fully to the work of
> the Lord, because you know that your labor in the Lord
> is not in vain.
>
> 1 Corinthians 15:58

God doesn't call all of us to missions—at least not in the sense of going to a foreign country. But the verse above reminds us that he does *give* each of us a mission. We are to give ourselves fully to the work of the Lord. Your work may be to represent Christ in the business world, or to use a gift or talent he has given you to glorify his kingdom, or to help people at your local mission or crisis pregnancy center.

Whatever work the Lord intends us to do, he expects us to stand firm and let nothing get in its way. The verse above says that our labor in the Lord is not in vain. That implies that everything else we do outside of God's intentions is done in vain. So if we want to give ourselves fully to the work he's called us to do, we will use the gifts and talents he's given us *now* and not wait for some future opportunity that may or may not ever materialize.

Many singles are free to work long hours, travel wherever God may lead, and respond to the needs of people instantly. Those who are married may not have such luxuries, and therefore God sometimes uses singles to accomplish specific tasks in his plan, tasks he doesn't use married people to do.

Seek God intensely to discover why he has given you the free time you enjoy. We have the privilege of serving

God wholeheartedly right now. We may never have such opportunities again.

Whatever God has given you to do, let nothing move you. Persevere and receive the blessings and joy that come from serving the Lord.

1. What work has the Lord given you to which he expects you to commit yourself fully?

2. How faithful have you been in completing that work?

3. How has your longing for love interfered with that work?

4. Do you agree that if you don't use your singleness right now the way God intends, you are spending your time in vain? Explain.

5. List all of the benefits that your singleness brings to the task(s) that God has given you to accomplish.

Part 6

God's Timing

If we're waiting for a change in our lives—whether a new job, a desired move, a promotion, or a relationship—we'll point to almost anything except God's timing as the reason it hasn't yet happened. If only we had landed the big deal, or if only we were not so shy or insecure, or if only we could figure out where to meet good Christian singles, then we would have what seems constantly out of reach.

None of these reasons, however, leaves room for God's handiwork in the lives of other people. God may intend for us to marry someone whom he wants to mature in the faith before bringing him or her across our path. He may intend for you to get that new job, but he hasn't worked out the details yet. He may intend a thousand other scenarios.

He also may need to make some changes in our lives. Maybe he's been prompting us to get our financial house in order or conquer a besetting sin. No amount of fighting against his timing or seeking a way around it will work. We really wouldn't want it to, would we? He knows the plans he has for us. Resting in that fact can be a source of great peace.

No matter which area of life we seek to discern God's timing, doing so requires us to be close enough to hear him when he speaks to us. It also requires good discernment skills that the Holy Spirit supplies only after we've immersed ourselves in the Word.

Waiting for God can be sobering, but it is never passive. As we repent of our sins and study our Bibles, we should be "out there" looking for a spouse if we desire one. We should pursue career opportunities, new places to live, and ministry opportunities. Pursuit is our job. Making things happen is God's.

For the next ten days, we will study the concept of God's timing. We'll look at specific examples of God's timing from Scripture and determine whether we trust his timing or our own works.

51

Finding Love in a Harvest Field

> Boaz replied, "I've been told all about what you have
> done for your mother-in-law since the death of your hus-
> band—how you left your father and mother and your
> homeland and came to live with a people you did not
> know before."
>
> Ruth 2:11

After the death of Naomi's husband and then her sons,
she encouraged both her daughters-in-law to return to
their mother's home. Naomi wanted them to find husbands.
Yet one of her daughters-in-law, Ruth, refused to leave
Naomi's side. She wanted to return to Judah with Naomi
to care for her, and she wanted to integrate into the society
of believers with Naomi.

When they got to Judah, Ruth heard about Boaz, a
wealthy relative of Naomi's husband, who owned a field
of grain. According to Deuteronomy 24:19, when a person harvested his fields, he was not to go back and pick
up the harvest that fell to the ground. That harvest was
instead to be reserved for the stranger, the fatherless, and
the widow.

So Ruth asked Naomi if she could go to this relative's
field to gather some food. I won't pretend to tell you that
Ruth didn't have ulterior motives. According to Ruth 2:2,
she wanted to catch the eye of this relative, and Naomi later
encouraged her to do exactly that (3:3). Ruth didn't know
yet whether he was in line as her kinsman-redeemer, but
she wanted to investigate.

Look at Ruth 2:11 to find out what impressed Boaz
about Ruth. She had a reputation for caring for Naomi.

Ruth could have let Naomi return to Judah alone—it certainly wouldn't have been wrong for her to do so—but she believed it was her responsibility to care for Naomi. So she was faithful to do what she thought she should do, and in the process, God brought her into contact with Boaz, whom she eventually married.

If you and I stay faithful to what we believe God wants us to do, he may have Mr. or Ms. Right in the next harvest field. But we can't find love in a harvest field if we don't show up.

DIGGING DEEPER INTO RUTH 2:11

1. Name one instance when you experienced God's perfect timing.

2. How was God's timing perfect in Ruth's case? Explain.

3. How was Ruth's faithfulness to care for Naomi connected to God bringing Boaz into her life?

4. Name one specific thing you know God has called you to do (care for an elderly parent, change jobs, start a business, and so on).

5. Look back at your answer in the last question. How faithful have you been to pursue what you wrote down?

52

Compelled to Action?

> "You acted foolishly," Samuel said. "You have not kept the command the LORD your God gave you; if you had, he would have established your kingdom over Israel for all time."
>
> 1 Samuel 13:13

The prophet Samuel instructed King Saul to go to Gilgal and wait seven days until Samuel arrived to sacrifice burnt offerings and fellowship offerings (1 Samuel 10)—an easy enough command to follow, you may think. However, in Gilgal, a war was brewing between the Philistines and Israel. The Philistines had three thousand chariots, six thousand charioteers, and soldiers as numerous as the sand on the seashore (1 Sam. 13:5). Israel had three thousand men.

As his troops quaked with fear, Saul waited seven days for Samuel to show up. On the seventh day, with his troops beginning to scatter, Saul made the burnt offering and fellowship offering. Then Samuel appeared and rebuked the king for not waiting as God had instructed him to.

Saul's intentions were good. He wanted to make sure that Israel sought the Lord's favor before going to war, but his fear led him to take action that God didn't authorize. He felt "compelled" to make the sacrifice (1 Sam. 13:12), although he wasn't a priest—the only people allowed by God to make sacrifices.

As easy as it is to look down on Saul for the actions he took, I wonder how many times we do similar things in our careers. God clearly leads us to a job. After being in that position awhile, we start to think about moving to another company or trying a new profession, yet at the same time we can't shake the feeling that God wants us to remain where we are—at least for now.

God doesn't always keep us in the same place; sometimes he leads us to move on. But when he doesn't, we feel like Saul did—compelled to action—don't we? And like Saul, we justify our action by saying that surely God would not want us to continue working in such a (fill in the blank) environment. Study 1 Samuel 13:13 again to determine what God thinks of such action.

DIGGING DEEPER INTO 1 SAMUEL 13:13

1. Do you think God was testing Saul by telling him to wait seven days for Samuel? Why or why not?

2. How important was the seven-day time period God set for Saul (read 1 Sam. 13:13–14)?

3. Do you believe that God guides and directs us in our jobs as he did with King Saul? Explain.

4. In the past, how have you felt compelled to take action into your own hands regarding your career?

5. What can you do to make sure you don't take matters into your own hands in the future regarding your career?

53

No Unfinished Packages

> Therefore, prepare your minds for action; be self-controlled;
> set your hope fully on the grace to be given you when Jesus
> Christ is revealed.
>
> 1 Peter 1:13

When Melanie's husband died after twenty years of marriage, she was unprepared for single life at the age of forty-three and didn't want to face life alone. "After he died, I wanted to get married by the end of that year, to resurrect that feeling of safety and reliability," Melanie remembered. "It didn't happen."

She entered into a relationship with a man after her husband died, but she soon found out this man adamantly refused to get married again. His spouse had also died, and he chose to deal with his pain differently than Melanie did. He didn't want to be close to anyone else.

Melanie now has many questions about her future. "Will I have a husband? Who will it be? How will I know? Will I be single for the rest of my life? Can I do that well, and gracefully?"

None of us can answer such questions, but Melanie has drawn tremendous strength from the Scriptures. One of the verses that has sustained her is the verse above. First Peter 1:13 doesn't allow for passivity but rather commands us to prepare our minds for action. It doesn't allow us to "do our own thing" but rather calls us to be self-controlled. Finally, it doesn't allow us to place our ultimate hope in external things but rather to set our hope on the grace we will receive when Jesus is revealed.

Melanie knows that God is always at work and in control of her future. "I don't want an unfinished package! I don't want a rush job! I want the timing to be just right, and I can wait as long as it takes."

DIGGING DEEPER INTO 1 PETER 1:13

1. Have you ever wondered, as Melanie did, what your future holds?

2. List three tasks you know God has given you to accomplish right now.

3. How can you prepare your mind so you can focus on those tasks and not on your concerns for the future?

4. Is your hope set more on external circumstances or on God's grace?

5. How does Melanie's insight about not wanting an unfinished package help you trust God's timing a little more?

54

Our Timing Stinks

I wait for the LORD, my soul waits,
and in his word I put my hope.

Psalm 130:5

God's timing often can be difficult to understand. I have a friend whom I will call Mandy. We respect each other. We know each other's personality. We are comfortable with each other. I even think if we spent enough time together, things could work between us. But the timing has never been right.

Most of our attempts to become a couple occurred before we became Christians in our midtwenties. We had no spiritual discernment whatsoever during those attempts, and I'm not surprised that things didn't work out. We did try one more time after becoming Christians, but frankly, neither of us was mature enough in the faith to trust God and his timing for our relationship.

We've often joked about how much our timing stinks. I no longer believe that our timing was bad in a negative sense, but rather in the sense that apparently God doesn't intend for us to be together—at least not yet. In the verse above, the psalmist put his hope in the Lord's Word. Mandy and I would have saved ourselves some emotional pain if we had put our hope in his Word and waited for him to speak to us rather than just trying to make it work like we did.

However, I don't believe that waiting on God means that we as singles should be passive when it comes to finding a spouse. Actually I believe quite the opposite. We need to be active in seeking a spouse if we desire one, but at the same time, we need to be sensitive to God's leading and guiding voice during each step of the process.

As we are sensitive to his leading, and as our souls wait for him, our hope will be rooted in his Word, not a possible love interest.

DIGGING DEEPER INTO PSALM 130:5

1. Have you ever been in a situation similar to Mandy's and mine? Explain.

2. When things didn't work out, what did you blame as the cause?

3. How often did you think about the aspect of God's timing while you were going through the pain of things not working out?

4. How willing are you to accept God's timing now regarding your marital status?

5. Does accepting God's timing regarding your marital status comfort you or frighten you? Explain.

55

Preparing to Go

> Then after three years, I went up to Jerusalem to get
> acquainted with Peter and stayed with him fifteen days.
>
> Galatians 1:18

Jessica has always had a passion for missions. "It eats at
me night and day," says the twenty-five-year-old. "Ever
since I was a little girl, missions has always appealed to me.
I just want God to fling me all over the planet for him.

"Every time I open the Bible," she says, "I long to do
what the men and women on the pages of the New Testament did. They lived solely for God. They did what God
told them to do." Yet as much as she had dreamed about
missions, she never felt called to go.

God changed all that during a worship service in Sep-
tember 2003. Jessica came away with a clear calling to go.
She is currently trying to remove all self-made obstacles so
she can be prepared to leave as soon as God tells her when
and where to go.

"It's about overcoming *me* right now," she says. "Dying
to my flesh, laying down my pride, setting my fear aside.
These things are taking time, and God is using this time
to sharpen me, to ready me, to grow me . . . all so he can
use me."

As much as she realizes how necessary this time of preparation is, Jessica understandably also wants to meet needs
right now. We aren't told in the first chapter of Galatians
whether the apostle Paul felt this way or not during his
three years in Arabia and Damascus. We do know that it
was necessary for him to get away with God for an extended
period of time before God sent him to the mission field.

People will always have needs, whether in countries far away or in the office cubicle next to us. Only God knows how and, just as importantly, when to meet those needs in the context of his sovereign plans. Our job is to spend extended time with him and trust his timing to meet those needs.

DIGGING DEEPER INTO GALATIANS 1:18

1. How would you rate your passion to meet people's needs?

2. How quick have you been to jump into action without spending time with God?

3. Do you ever think about God's timing when it comes to meeting people's needs? Explain.

4. If you had to wait for three years as the apostle Paul did before he could go to the mission field to which God called him, would you consider it a waste of time?

5. How will this verse help you to deal with times of preparation in the future?

56

In God's Perfect Timing

Jacob was in love with Rachel and said, "I'll work for you
seven years in return for your younger daughter Rachel."

Genesis 29:18

Have you ever met someone at a social gathering and the sparks flew? You noticed not only the color of that person's eyes but also the sparkle in his or her eyes that seemed to invite you to explore that person more deeply. That's what happened between Jacob and Rachel. Genesis 29:17 says that Rachel was lovely in form and beautiful. Jacob fell so hard for her that he was willing to work for her father for seven years just to marry her.

If you were presented with Jacob's situation, would you have worked for seven years for the one you loved? Think back to what you were doing seven years ago. Were you working at the same job you are now? Attending the same church? Courting the same person? Our lives change a lot over a seven-year period, don't they?

Imagine what Rachel must have felt like. She found the man she wanted to marry and then had to be around him often over the next seven years without being able to marry him. She must have struggled with doubts about whether they would ever marry. Then, when the time finally arrived, she must have been devastated to find out that her father had tricked the man she loved into marrying her sister, Leah.

What Rachel could not possibly have understood at the time was that God would eventually bring the Savior of the world through the bloodline of Jacob and Leah. Jesus descended from a marriage that was based on deceit—at least on an earthly level—but God had bigger plans. Rachel eventually married Jacob in God's perfect timing.

God is orchestrating events in our lives to bring himself glory. Like Rachel, we don't know God's timing for our future, but we can trust that just as he knew what he was doing with Rachel, he knows what he is doing with us.

DIGGING DEEPER INTO GENESIS 29:18

1. Have you ever fallen in love with somebody only to have God tell you to wait for marriage?

2. Did you question God's timing? Explain.

3. What did you do during this period of waiting?

4. Did you ever think about the big picture? That God was at work orchestrating the events of your life for his glory? Or were you more self-focused? Explain.

5. How can this verse change the way you handle future relationships if God tells you to wait for marriage?

57

Time to Move?

Since ancient times no one has heard,
   no ear has perceived,
no eye has seen any God besides you,
   who acts on behalf of those who wait for him.
You come to the help of those who gladly do right,
   who remember your ways.

Isaiah 64:4–5

Chongsun has been considering a move from the West Coast to the East Coast for the past two years. "I hear from friends who have lived on the East Coast that it's quite different from the West Coast," says the single twenty-five-year-old. "So I've always been curious about going to places like New York or Boston, especially since I've never even visited these places."

Currently he lives in what he calls "West Coast suburbia." He wants to move to a more urban area on the East Coast. Beyond his curiosity for a new culture, Chongsun believes God could use his move to grow his faith in many ways. "Like knowing how to adapt to new surroundings, or having a heart for urban poor, or diversifying my perspective from meeting people with different views than myself. These will all be beneficial if I am serious about wanting to advance God's kingdom throughout the world, where cultures are very different from the United States."

He has hesitated to move for one reason: "It didn't seem to be the right time, as I still felt there were things God wanted to teach me in my current season of life." Only recently has he sensed that God's timing for his move may be closing in. Not wanting to misinterpret God's timing,

Chongsun remains in prayer about this and takes intermediate practical steps, such as investigating potential living areas on the East Coast and applying to seminary in these locations, knowing that God is in control.

This passage from Isaiah encourages action on our part. It also encourages us to wait on God. How do we do both at the same time? Live for God first, continue to seek his will, and wait upon him for the results—just as Chongsun is doing.

1. What is your normal thought process when you are considering a move?

2. How important is God's timing to you when considering a move?

3. Have you ever sensed God telling you that the timing is not right for a move? Explain.

4. According to these verses, we should be in the practice of waiting on him while at the same time remaining active. Does that describe you when you consider a move?

5. What can you do to make sure you don't misinterpret God's timing the next time you consider a move?

58

Not Now

> Then the word of the LORD came to me: "You must not
> marry and have sons or daughters in this place."
>
> Jeremiah 16:1–2

Jeremiah was a single man who wasn't well liked among his own people because God had assigned him the task of warning Judah about impending judgment if they did not repent. But despite his difficult task, Jeremiah wasn't alone. God's hand was on him before he was even born (Jer. 1:5).

Knowing that God was with him, imagine how he must have felt when God told him that he wasn't supposed to get married and have children in Judah. Notice, however, that God didn't tell Jeremiah he could never marry; he just told him he couldn't marry "in this place."

God was gracious enough to explain why Jeremiah could not marry in Judah. In Jeremiah 16:4, God said, "They will die of deadly diseases. . . . They will perish by sword and famine." In other words, God didn't want Jeremiah to marry because God was about to judge Judah and didn't want to kill Jeremiah's family.

God's timing wasn't right for Jeremiah to start a family—even though he was lonely (Jer. 15:17) and apparently wanted to marry. God had work for Jeremiah to do, and that work did not include a family. It would have been easy for Jeremiah to complain or ask God to give him a family and then protect them, but he didn't do that.

Instead, look at Jeremiah's first words in response to God: "Oh LORD, my strength and my fortress, my refuge in time of distress, to you the nations will come from the ends of the earth" (Jer. 16:19). Jeremiah wasn't focused on himself and what he was "missing out on"; rather, he saw God's purpose in his singleness—to call the people of his nation to repentance.

God's timing for us is always perfect. Jeremiah had a job to do for God. So do we. It may not include calling a nation back to God, but whatever his plans are for us, they are equally important.

DIGGING DEEPER INTO JEREMIAH 16:1-2

1. How fearful are you that God might tell you not to marry for a period of time, as he did with Jeremiah?

2. How would you have responded to God if you had been in Jeremiah's place?

3. If God chooses to never explain this season of singleness to you, how can you show him that you trust him anyway?

4. Which do you think about the most often—your future or what God wants you to do today?

5. List three gifts or talents God has given you. How can you use them more effectively this month?

59

When It Is Not Our Time

Yet no one seized him, because his time had not yet come.

John 8:20

As Jesus spoke to a crowd of people on the Mount of Olives, the Pharisees challenged his claims about who he was by saying that his testimony about himself was invalid because no one else corroborated his story. They referred to Deuteronomy 17:6 and 19:15, which disallow a person from being convicted of a crime without the testimony of at least two witnesses.

Jesus said that his Father had sent him, and therefore he had two witnesses. When the Pharisees asked where his Father was, he said they did not know him. Perhaps the Pharisees were thinking about Jesus's earthly father during their line of questioning, but surely by this point in his ministry, they had heard him claim that he came from his Father in heaven (John 6:44).

Their possible confusion aside, they were feeling threatened by Jesus and, according to the verse above, were already thinking about ways to stop him. "Yet no one seized him, because his time had not yet come." Even Jesus's ministry was subject to God's timing. In this case, his ministry was leading up to his crucifixion, but many of the Old Testament prophecies had not yet been fulfilled regarding Jesus. So he would not complete his earthly ministry until God worked everything out.

In the meantime, Jesus had more people to heal, more teaching to do, more preparation of his disciples for what would come. Knowing "his time had not yet come," he continued on with his immediate ministry.

You and I sometimes get frustrated when we try to get involved in some new sort of ministry and the timing just isn't right. But if Jesus had to wait until God's timing was perfect, how much more do we need to wait. His actions should be a great encouragement for us the next time we see that God's timing is not right for the ministry we desire, and it also will help us stay active in the ministry he has already given us.

DIGGING DEEPER INTO JOHN 8:20

1. What ministry have you wanted to join or begin, but the timing just hasn't seemed to be right?

2. Have you wondered if you could do something to make it happen, but you haven't been able to figure out what? Explain.

3. How has John 8:20 changed your mind about why things haven't worked out with this ministry?

4. What effect will this have on your attitude toward this ministry?

5. How can you stay active in ministry while waiting on God's timing?

60

On Being a Chicken

As the heavens are higher than the earth,
so are my ways higher than your ways
and my thoughts than your thoughts.

Isaiah 55:9

Scott knows what it feels like to continually wonder how much longer God wants him to wait for a spouse. "I know I shouldn't question God's will for any aspect of my life, but at twenty-seven, my curiosity about his plan continues to surface," Scott said. "Why have I come this far and still remain so single? I've never even been in a serious relationship! Why? Of course I know it simply isn't my time, but it's so hard not to wonder why."

While Scott knows what it feels like to ask the "why" question, he is also aware that God's ways are indeed not his ways. In fact, he has even considered how God may be using Scott's flawed character traits. "As I look back at times in my past when I had the chance to get involved with someone, it almost seems as if God made me in such a way that I would never get close to a relationship until he wanted me to. It's actually rather amusing," Scott explained. "He blessed me with the unfortunate (and, at times, fortunate) trait of being a chicken. I've just never had the guts to ask a girl out."[6]

I think Scott is on to something. Of course, our character traits don't give us license to disobey God. In Scott's case, if God prompted him to do something that he felt too shy to act upon, then he would be in sin. But at the same time, God created Scott as a shy person for a reason. Scott may have stumbled onto that reason.

The fact is, God can and does use everything to accomplish his will. And since his ways are higher than ours, we cannot discount him using our own character traits to orchestrate his plan for our lives.

1. Scott knows that God's timing just hasn't been right yet for him to marry, but he still wonders why. In what ways can you relate to his struggle?

2. Which character traits do you have that God might be using in his timing for providing you with a spouse?

3. In what ways may God be using those character traits in his timing for providing you with a spouse?

4. Do you trust God to provide the grace to overcome those traits when his timing is perfect for you to find a spouse?

5. Write a prayer thanking God for the way he made you. Express your trust of him to give you the grace to overcome any deficiencies you may have when the time is right.

Part 7

No Fair!

When I was in my early to midtwenties, several of my friends got married. As I attended one wedding after another, I noticed an attitude that began to burrow its way into my mind and finally into my heart: *This isn't fair. Everyone else is getting married but me.*

I wasn't a Christian when I first noticed this attitude, but even after I became a Christian, I struggled with the concept of fairness. It seems absurd on the surface. We all know that God is fair and just, but seeing somebody get something that we desperately desire can raise feelings of covetousness. It just didn't seem fair.

My concept of fairness said that everybody is supposed to get the exact same thing—much like a child who screams when he or she doesn't get the same size piece of cake as his or her sibling. When many of my friends got married, I was sure I wouldn't be far behind them. I was wrong.

What I didn't understand at the time was that my understanding of fairness wasn't even close to the biblical concept. I didn't even know that there was a biblical concept of fairness. But thankfully, in God's mercy and patience, he sent me to the Scriptures for examples of fairness.

What I found changed my entire perception of fairness. I no longer believe God owes marriage to me and that it would be unfair of him if he didn't give it to me.

For the next ten days, we will examine the Scriptures with regard to fairness. Your struggle with this issue may not be related to marriage but about other singles who are purchasing homes, or someone who got that high-paying job you always wanted, or maybe even married people who get benefits at work that you don't. No matter how you struggle with the concept of fairness, put your view of it aside and let God's Word speak to you and change you.

61

A Healthy Dose of Fear

> Great and marvelous are your deeds,
>> Lord God Almighty.
> Just and true are your ways,
>> King of the ages.
> Who will not fear you, O Lord,
>> and bring glory to your name?
> For you alone are holy.

Revelation 15:3–4

On December 7, 2002, I walked down the aisle, but on my friend Herb's arm rather than my daddy's," Gail told me recently. "I wasn't walking to meet my elusive husband but to stand as a bridesmaid for the fifth time in my life."

In the verses above, the saints in heaven sing a song praising God for who he is and for his ways. Knowing God's holiness, knowing God is just and true, they sing praises to him instead of objecting to his plans. They have a proper view of fairness.

The older we get as singles, the more we see friends and loved ones walk down the aisle. The more often it happens, the easier it is to feel as if life isn't fair. We've been faithful to God. We don't sleep around. We go to church. We love God. But without a potential spouse on the horizon, we think God is being unfair. All of us, including Gail, know that God can never be unfair, but our feelings often betray us.

Seems a little silly in light of how the saints in heaven will respond to God's justice, doesn't it? Granted, they are with God, which means their view of his fairness and justice is perfected. That perfected view starts with a question they will ask in their song: "Who will not fear you, O Lord, and bring glory to your name?"

The next time we are tempted to feel that God is unfair by allowing someone we know to marry while we remain single, a healthy dose of the fear of God will go a long way toward changing our attitude.

DIGGING DEEPER INTO REVELATION 15:3-4

1. Describe what you felt the last time you struggled with feelings of unfairness during a friend or relative's wedding.

2. How could it be possible for God to be just and true while at the same time your current marital status is unfair?

3. What three things did the saints focus on in these two verses?

4. How would turning your own focus on these things help you the next time you struggle with feelings of unfairness when a friend gets married?

5. In your understanding, what does "fear of the Lord" mean?

62

The Lord Is Our Portion

> Then the LORD said to Aaron: "You shall have no inheritance in their land, nor shall you have any portion among them; I am your portion and your inheritance among the children of Israel."
>
> Numbers 18:20 NKJV

Before Israel ever crossed into the Promised Land of Canaan, God had a plan for the way he wanted the land divided among the twelve tribes of Israel. He also made it clear in the verse above that the tribe of Levi—from Aaron to all the priests—would not receive any land once they reached Canaan. God was to be their portion and inheritance.

An outsider might have deemed that situation unfair. After all, shouldn't the priests—the representatives of God to his people—be given more than anybody else? How could it be fair for them to receive no land? As is always the case when we try to judge what is fair and what isn't by human standards, we are left with questions like these. Humans compare portions—in this case, land—and deem the giver unfair if everybody doesn't receive the same amount. God doesn't work that way.

Some singles may feel like the tribe of Levi. They don't have any land (or housing) of their own. Maybe you are unable to afford a home or nice apartment by yourself. For most of my adult life, I have lived with roommates to keep expenses down. Regardless of our current housing situation, some of our single friends have bigger or nicer houses or apartments than we do. With that comes the temptation to consider this inequitable and unfair.

Just as God had a different purpose for the tribe of Levi than for the other tribes, God has different purposes for you and me. Therefore, our housing situation will be different. That does not make it unfair; rather, it is the portion that God has given to us right now, and nothing can ever be unfair about the portions God gives us.

DIGGING DEEPER INTO NUMBERS 18:20

1. In the past, when you read Numbers 18:20, did it seem unfair to you that the tribe of Levi wouldn't receive any land while the rest of the tribes of Israel did? Explain.

2. How has this devotion helped you to see fairness from a different perspective?

3. Before reading this devotion, how did you view your current housing situation?

4. What do you think God's purpose is for your current housing situation?

5. What does God mean when he says he will be your portion? Read Lamentations 3:24; Psalms 16:5; 73:26; 119:57; and Jeremiah 10:16 before you answer.

63

The Demands of Our Sin Nature

> You diligently study the Scriptures because you think that
> by them you possess eternal life. These are the Scriptures
> that testify about me, yet you refuse to come to me to
> have life.
>
> John 5:39–40

I f you have ever tried to share the Good News with someone who was not a believer, then you've heard such re-
marks as, "Christianity is too narrow-minded. I believe that
all religions are equal and that all of them eventually lead
to God" and "If Jesus is the only way to heaven, then what
about the people who live in areas of the world that have
never heard his name? Are you telling me that those people
will go to hell when they die?"

Jesus faced people with the same attitude. In John 5, the
Jews questioned Jesus about why he healed a man on the
Sabbath. When Jesus equated himself with God (v. 17), and
therefore as the Lord of the Sabbath, the Jews sought to
kill him. Yet that didn't stop Jesus from telling them that
the Old Testament Scriptures, which they had "diligently"
studied, testified about him being the way to eternal life.
In all of the time they had spent studying the Scriptures,
they had failed to grasp the main point.

People's inherent sinful nature wants to earn salvation
by doing enough good works. The idea that someone who
doesn't perform as many good works as we do will go to
heaven simply because that person believes that Jesus died
for his or her sins doesn't seem fair. Whenever a person
thinks that to be the case, he has put his own view of fairness on a higher standard than God's view.

We shouldn't be surprised when unbelievers reject God's offer of salvation because they see his way as too narrow. Apart from God's Spirit opening their eyes, their sinful nature rules them and their sin nature demands "fairness" as their flesh understands it. But as believers, we are to consider our sinful nature as dead and look to God and his Word for direction in every area of life. When we find ourselves struggling with anything being "fair" or not—from our housing arrangement, to our job situation, to our marital status—it is a good indication that we are allowing our sinful nature to rule our lives.

DIGGING DEEPER INTO JOHN 5:39-40

1. When you share the Good News, how often do you hear comments from unbelievers about Christianity being too narrow?

2. What is your normal response?

3. How often do you encounter people who believe they can earn their salvation by being "good" or by being better than other people?

4. What role do you believe their concept of fairness plays in thinking about salvation?

5. Write one response that you can use in the future that might turn people's thoughts from their concept of fairness toward the holiness of God regarding their salvation.

64

Why Those Twelve?

> One of those days Jesus went out to a mountainside to pray, and spent the night praying to God. When morning came, he called his disciples to him and chose twelve of them, whom he also designated apostles.
>
> Luke 6:12–13

After a full night in prayer, Jesus called his disciples ("a great number of people"—Luke 6:17) together and then chose twelve of them as apostles. Imagine standing in the crowd of Jesus's disciples. For those of us who would want to be chosen, think about the emotions you would feel as Jesus called the twelfth name and your name was not among them.

Now throw into the mix several facts that you couldn't possibly have known while standing there but that Jesus already knew. One of the Twelve would deny him, one would doubt him, and one would betray him. Jesus chose them anyway.

If you had known what Jesus did, how would you have reacted? Maybe pointed out their eventual flaws? Maybe made a case for yourself because of your loyalty? Maybe you wouldn't have said anything, but you would have struggled to see how Jesus could have been fair in choosing people who wouldn't be loyal to him.

In reality Jesus didn't choose the twelve that he did because they deserved it. He chose them after spending all night in prayer with the Father. God had a plan for his Son—right down to the way he would die and the people who would be with him.

When somebody else gets recognition at work or church, it is easy to feel as if God isn't fair to us. Why did he choose that person and not us? We did as much work. We may have even come up with the idea in the first place. We put in long hours, but God chose that other person for recognition instead.

Just as God wasn't unfair when he guided Jesus in choosing the twelve apostles, he isn't unfair when he chooses someone else for recognition. He just has different plans for us right now. Different does not mean unfair in God's economy.

DIGGING DEEPER INTO LUKE 6:12–13

1. Have you ever considered the methodology Jesus used when choosing the twelve apostles as unfair? Explain.

2. What did Jesus's twelve apostles do to warrant being chosen?

3. Why do you think there wasn't an outcry of unfairness from the multitude of disciples who weren't chosen?

4. Based on your answer from the previous question, how should we handle feelings of unfairness the next time they threaten to overwhelm us?

5. How is your perspective of God's fairness starting to change now that you see Scriptures such as this one that assume God is always fair as he orchestrates his plans for his people?

65

Promotion Comes from God

> For not from the east nor from the west nor from the
> south come promotion and lifting up. But God is the
> Judge! He puts down one and lifts up another.
>
> Psalm 75:6–7 AMP

Laura used to work with a man who left to take a new position outside of the company. Within months he came back. Upon his return, he was promoted and given a new job title with a higher salary.

"Somehow he got promoted," she said, "(even) though he was the one who left, and here I was, with seniority and doing a good job and staying, and I wasn't getting any of those benefits." She did not get over the situation quickly.

"I wish I could say I wasn't resentful," she said. "I wish I could say that this didn't affect my morale at work. But it did. I spent much time complaining to co-workers and to God about the unfairness of it all. However, I finally realized it was eating away at me most days and also affecting the way I related to my boss."

She knew she needed to do something. "I had always heard that promotion ultimately comes from God," so she decided to trust the truth of that verse. "Gradually I was able to completely let it go. That is when the peace returned. I am now at peace with this individual and my boss. And I know that my boss sees what I do and so does God."

In addition to the verse above, she says that Psalm 5:12 also helped her deal with feelings of unfairness about her co-worker's promotion. "Lord, you bless those who do what is right; you protect them like a soldier's shield" (NCV).

"Doing the right thing in this case is being thankful in all circumstances," she said. "It is speaking well of our neighbor and not bearing false witness. It is in speaking highly and not in slandering a co-worker. And then when we let it go, get off our soapbox, and graciously hand over the reins to the Lord, seeking to be under his control, he says that he protects us."

DIGGING DEEPER INTO PSALM 75:6-7

1. Name the last person who was promoted at work who was less qualified than you were.

2. How did you handle the situation?

3. If God really determines who is promoted, why do we still feel slighted in cases like this?

4. How does this verse change your perspective about the concept of promotion?

5. If you are at a point where you can thank God for promoting the person you listed in the first question instead of you, do so here.

66

I Am Supposed to Get Married First!

> He is the Rock, his works are perfect,
> and all his ways are just.
> A faithful God who does no wrong,
> upright and just is he.

> Deuteronomy 32:4

When she was twenty-four, her twenty-year-old sister got married, and Amy felt devastated. "I am the oldest sister," Amy remarked, recalling the event. "I am supposed to be the one who gets married first! I felt sorry for myself for a long time after that, and I am ashamed to admit I spent a good deal of time being angry at God for allowing things to happen that way."

Amy's sister got married nine years ago. Amy continued to pray for a spouse after her sister's wedding, but recently she realized something about those prayers. "I have been praying all along, but the majority of my prayers have been very selfish," Amy said. "I have wanted immediate answers, and unfortunately God doesn't work that way."

She recently went through a breakup with her fiancé, and it changed her prayer life. Only after the breakup did she "start praying for God's will and not my own to be done." That's one of the most difficult prayers to pray when you yearn for something as significant as a spouse. Amy reached the point where she was willing to trust God's ways above her own. The journey took her nine years to complete, but I suspect she completed it faster than many of us will.

When we question God about his fairness regarding any part of our lives, we deny the truth of Deuteronomy 32:4.

Let's look at the verse a little more in depth. If "all his ways are just," then his timing can't possibly be unfair. If he is "a faithful God who does no wrong," then he's a personal God who is faithful and fair to us in all circumstances. Even when we watch other—sometimes younger—people walk down the aisle before us.

DIGGING DEEPER INTO DEUTERONOMY 32:4

1. Describe the emotions you felt the last time you were angry that someone who was younger than you got married.

2. What motivated those feelings?

3. Have you confessed that motivation as sin? If not, take the time to do it now.

4. How close are you to reaching the point where you can honestly say that you accept God's will and that you will pray for his will regarding your life?

5. How will praying this way change your prayer life?

67

God's Things, God's Way

Is it not lawful for me to do what I wish with my own things?

Matthew 20:15 NKJV

In recent years, newspapers and websites have been publishing articles about singles complaining about unfair treatment by their employers. They point to "domestic partnership" benefits (of both the homosexual and heterosexual variety), sick leave, and time off for co-workers with children; day-care benefits for co-workers with children; being forced to work holidays and weekends while those who are married do not have to; and several other perceived inequities.

The workers in the parable of the vineyard (Matt. 20:1–16) felt as if they weren't being treated fairly either. All of the workers started working at different times of the day, and at the end of the day, they were all paid the wages they had agreed upon individually with the landowner. When they found out they all received the same amount of money, they were upset and accused the landowner of treating them unfairly. The first time I read this parable, I nodded my head in agreement with them.

It is easy to miss whom the landowner represents. At the beginning of this parable (Matt. 20:1), Jesus likened the kingdom of heaven to the landowner who hired these laborers for his vineyard. The landowner is God. In the verse above, the landowner asked a simple yet profound question: "Is it not lawful for me to do what I wish with my own things?"

Biblical fairness has nothing to do with making sure we receive the same wage for the same amount of hours as our co-workers. Our employers do not owe us that. Nor does it have anything to do with making sure we receive the same benefits as our co-workers. They do not owe us that either. They do owe us the benefits that we agreed to when we took the position, just as we owe them an honest day's work for the wage we agreed to when we started. This is the difference between the world's definition of fairness and the Bible's.

DIGGING DEEPER INTO MATTHEW 20:15

1. Describe your attitude the last time a married person in your office received a benefit at work that you do not normally receive.

2. Why did you think it was unfair?

3. When reading the parable of the workers in the vineyard in the past, have you sided with the workers in their claim of unfairness or with the landowner? Explain.

4. Based on this parable, what would fairness in the workplace look like regarding benefits and wages?

5. How has this passage given you a fresh understanding about fairness?

68

Why Can't I Look Like That?

I praise you because I am fearfully and wonderfully
made;
your works are wonderful,
I know that full well.

Psalm 139:14

I have been overweight since I was a child. When I was in high school, I was an avid tennis player, and though I played five or six hours a day during the summer, I was still overweight. No doubt some of it had to do with my eating habits, but I was eating the same things as everyone else my age. Food just affected me differently.

As I grew into adulthood, I began to wish I were more attractive. I've even gone so far as to think that it is unfair for some people to be more physically attractive than others. Why do some people garner the majority of attention from the opposite sex simply because they are more attractive than other people?

No matter how much we might say that attraction is not a factor when it comes to finding a spouse, it is not true—even for Christians. Most people are not going to enter a relationship with someone they are not drawn to physically, at least in some fashion. And how many times in the Scriptures does one unmarried person find another unmarried person attractive and then decide to pursue the possibility of a relationship leading to marriage? (See Gen. 6:2; 29:17; Deut. 21:11; Judg. 14:1; Song of Songs 1:8.)

Why didn't God create all of us to look exactly alike, or at least with an equal amount of attractiveness? Perhaps for the same reason that he didn't give us all the same gifts, talents, money, personal belongings, or jobs. It was simply not in his will.

Thankfully not everybody finds the same physical characteristics attractive, and after all, it takes only one person to find us attractive. To constantly stew about why we are not more attractive brings us dangerously close to denying the truth of Psalm 139:14. We are fearfully and wonderfully made by God. He doesn't make mistakes.

DIGGING DEEPER INTO PSALM 139:14

1. Describe your motivation for wanting to look differently than you do.

2. How much of a role do you believe physical appearance plays in bringing a man and woman together?

3. Explain why you believe that it is either right or wrong for physical appearance to be important in a relationship.

4. If you are treating your body like a temple, how is it possible that you don't look exactly the way God chose for you to look?

5. Does Psalm 139:14 cause you to rethink the way you view your physical appearance?

69

I Have No Answer

> Then the LORD answered Job out of the storm. He said:
> "Who is this that darkens my counsel
>   with words without knowledge?
> Brace yourself like a man;
>   I will question you,
>   and you shall answer me."
>
> Job 38:1–3

As Job's friends continually and presumptuously questioned him about what he might have done to invite God's judgment on himself, he began to doubt God. In chapter 31, Job pointed to his sexual purity, his honesty, his hospitality, his lack of faith in money, and his love for his enemies, and then he made this statement: "Oh, that I had someone to hear me! I sign now my defense—let the Almighty answer me; let my accuser put his indictment in writing" (Job 31:35).

Every time I read through the book of Job, I cringe at such brash statements, although I have no doubt that Job was far more patient than I would have been in similar circumstances. He was convinced God had treated him unfairly, and he wanted an answer. He demanded an answer. He received one.

Starting just after the verse above, all the way through the end of chapter 39, God asked Job dozens of questions that Job couldn't possibly answer. God wanted to know where Job was when he laid the earth's foundations. He wanted to know where he was when he made the sea and clouds and animals. He wanted to know where he was when he controlled the weather.

How similar is Job's demand to our own demand for an answer when we claim that God has treated us unfairly by not providing a spouse for us when he provides marriage for others? I wonder if we are putting ourselves in a position to have to brace ourselves so that God can question and demand an answer from us.

Job eventually provided the only answer he could with any validity: "I am unworthy—how can I reply to you? I put my hand over my mouth. I spoke once, but I have no answer—twice, but I will say no more" (Job 40:4–5).

Good advice, don't you think?

DIGGING DEEPER INTO JOB 38:1-3

1. Over what issue do you deserve to hear God say, "Who is this that darkens my counsel with words without knowledge?" because you have questioned God's fairness?

2. What did you say to God when you demanded an answer regarding something you considered unfair?

3. In what way does this type of attitude reveal a pride problem?

4. If God demanded that you answer all of the questions he asked Job in chapters 38–39, how would you respond?

5. How would you respond to these two questions that God asked Job in Job 40:8? "Would you discredit my justice? Would you condemn me to justify yourself?"

70

Whatever Pleases Him

> The LORD does whatever pleases him,
> in the heavens and on the earth,
> in the seas and all their depths.
>
> Psalm 135:6

Verses such as the one above make some people uncomfortable because they think God sounds like a dictator. But taken in the context of the rest of Scripture, God has left no doubt that he loves humans, even in all their flaws. He sent his own Son to die so humans could live eternally with him. With his plan to bring the gospel to the nations always at the forefront, he does whatever brings him pleasure.

Of course, God's pleasures are always pure and just and beyond the right of humans to question—a right we often violate when we don't understand events in our lives. If we disregard God's plan and what pleases him, we conclude that God is treating us unfairly.

Rather than being upset, a deeper look at this passage should bring us a tremendous amount of comfort. Look at the last part of the passage. In doing whatever pleases him in the seas and all their depths, God not only shows his authority over the sea but his love for everything in it. The creatures don't have the ability to question God's fairness about why one fish gets more than another or even why one fish eats another. But even if they did, they would be wrong to do so—much as we are wrong when we question his fairness to us.

If it pleases God to sustain the creatures of the sea, how much more does it please him to justly sustain those he created in his image? Jesus asked a similar question in Matthew 10:29–31: "Are not two sparrows sold for a penny? Yet not one of them will fall to the ground apart from the will of your Father. And even the very hairs of your head are all numbered. So don't be afraid; you are worth more than many sparrows."

DIGGING DEEPER INTO PSALM 135:6

1. Explain your emotions and thought process as you think about this verse.

2. How could God ever do something that pleases himself and it be unfair?

3. How much have you thought about God's concern for justice toward the creatures in the sea and the sparrows Jesus mentioned in Matthew 10?

4. If you "are worth more than many sparrows" as Jesus said, how much more do you think God will care for and be just toward you?

5. How might Psalm 135:6 help you overcome any sense of unfairness that you still harbor toward God?

Part 8

Expectations

We all had expectations growing up about what our lives would look like when we were older. Perhaps we expected to be married, with a nice house and 2.3 children running around by the time we reached a certain age. Or we expected an athletic scholarship or admission to an Ivy League university. As the years passed, some of our expectations probably changed. Maybe we realized that we really weren't a good enough athlete, singer, dancer, or actress to make a living from it, so we adjusted our expectations and those former dreams became hobbies.

Disappointment always follows unfulfilled expectations and can lead to an attitude of passivity. We float from one day to the next without any desire to live each day to its fullest.

Singles often confront the added expectation from friends or family that marriage will somehow make their lives complete. "You can't possibly be happy roaming around your apartment by yourself," we hear; or less subtle, "You don't want to die an old maid, do you?"

The intentions of those who express their expectations for us are usually good—they want us to be happy. That's why it is so difficult to ask them to back off. Occasionally their intentions aren't good but rather self-serving, and in those instances, we should take a stand.

How do we stop allowing feelings of expectation—our own and others'—from governing our lives? For the next ten days, we will study what the Bible says about expectations. If you are open to what it says about the topic, the source of your expectations will be radically changed.

71

Death Leads to Life

> Then Jesus said to his disciples, "If anyone would come after me, he must deny himself and take up his cross and follow me."
>
> Matthew 16:24

When I was seventeen, my mom went with me to a jeweler to help me pick out a promise ring for my girlfriend. On Valentine's Day 1983, I gave the ring to my girlfriend and she graciously accepted it. We would soon be husband and wife. I expected to graduate from high school, find a job, get married, and have children.

When my girlfriend and I broke up just before I graduated, I was rattled, but I still expected to find a job, find somebody else, get married, and have children. Before I knew it, I was in my twenties and no closer to marriage than when I was with my first girlfriend.

My expectations weighed heavily on me. I felt like a failure. I didn't see any sense in advancing my education, buying a home, or pursuing a career. After all, I had nobody to share my life with. I dropped out of college, started going to nightclubs, and withdrew inside myself.

I stayed there for six or seven years. Then Christ intervened, saving me from my sin and continually encouraging me to follow him. But early in my walk with him, I was confused. I knew that marriage was a good thing—ordained and blessed in the Scriptures. So when I read Matthew 16:24, I wondered if Jesus was really telling me to deny myself regarding my expectations for marriage. The more I thought about it, the more I realized he was. A cross only has one use—death.

Yet we serve a God who conquered death and is in the business of bringing the dead to life. When he resurrects a life, it is changed. Killing our desires and expectations, whatever they may be, is painful, but death is necessary for living a resurrected life the way God intends.

DIGGING DEEPER INTO MATTHEW 16:24

1. Describe your expectations when you graduated from high school or college.

2. How did you feel when your expectations were not met?

3. How do Jesus's words in Matthew 16:24 relate to your expectations?

4. How willing are you to deny your expectations in order to follow Christ?

5. How close are you at this point in your walk with Christ to accepting his plans for your life?

72

Our Expectations versus God's Plan

> "For I know the plans I have for you," declares the LORD, "plans to prosper you and not to harm you, plans to give you hope and a future."
>
> Jeremiah 29:11

My parents were young when I was born, and I always wanted to be a relatively young parent," Sarah said. Thirty-one now, early on she followed through with her desires and got married at the age of twenty-three. Three years later she was divorced. This wasn't what she expected.

"I envisioned myself with a couple of children and a home of our own by the time I was thirty," she said.

In Jeremiah 29:11, God tells us that he too had a plan for his people. We like to quote this verse about our own future. It brings us comfort to know that God's plans for us are good and that we will prosper. However, let's look at the context of the verse. In verse 10, God speaks to Judah, the people he exiled to Babylon, and tells them that the promises in the verse above will be fulfilled *after* they have been in Babylon for seventy years. Did you catch that?

The people of Judah lived most of their lives in captivity in a foreign country. Some of them even died while in captivity before God prospered his people. Like the people of Judah, we need to hear the reminder that God has plans to give us a hope and a future.

Sarah is now trying to determine God's plan for her life. She's looking into doing some volunteer work at a local crisis pregnancy center and working to develop her writing skills—neither of which was part of her original plans. But she can be confident in knowing that God knew what he was doing all along, and now that she is seeking to live sacrificially for God, she can be assured that God will prosper her in some fashion as he promised.

DIGGING DEEPER INTO JEREMIAH 29:11

1. Describe your feelings of regret if you have allowed your expectations of finding a spouse to cause you to either marry and divorce at a young age or get involved in relationships that were not healthy.

2. How often do you read Jeremiah 29:11, hoping that your future involves a spouse?

3. How does this devotion help you to understand the context of Jeremiah 29:11 better?

4. Name one thing you can do the next time you feel tempted to equate this verse only toward marriage.

5. If your expectations for finding a spouse are not met, how willing are you to believe that God knows your future and desires to give you hope?

73

The Problem with Expectations

In his heart a man plans his course,
but the LORD determines his steps.

Proverbs 16:9

The root of our expectations can be found in our desires. What starts as a desire slowly transforms into feelings of deservedness. Once we buy into that, we expect to have our desires met. So we start to make plans with our expectations in mind.

The above verse says that a man plans his course in his heart. The Scriptures are clear about the condition of human hearts. Jesus said that "out of men's hearts, come evil thoughts, sexual immorality, theft, murder, adultery, greed, malice, deceit, lewdness, envy, slander, arrogance and folly" (Mark 7:21–22).

Apart from God, then, our expectations are rooted in corrupted desires—desires that are so corrupted, we hate to think of ourselves the way Jesus describes us in Mark 7:21–22. Even with the best of intentions, you and I both have to admit that many of our desires are selfish. We want to feel the emotional and physical closeness of another person. We want more money or authority at work. We want a big-screen TV. We want, we want, we want.

In our want, we leave God's desires for our lives out of our expectations. He wants to bring us into the likeness of Jesus, but we are so focused on ourselves that we have difficulty seeing Jesus.

Rather than letting our expectations drive our actions, it would be much better for our spiritual condition to seek God's expectations. He doesn't hide them from us. He continually calls us to obey his ways while putting our own ways to death. We can rejoice in knowing that as we go about that difficult task, he will continually guide us.

1. To what extent have your expectations gradually become a sense of entitlement instead?

2. List two of your heart's biggest desires.

3. Read Mark 7:21–22. How might your answers from question 2 be skewed by a sinful heart?

4. How might you have placed too much faith in your heart in the past?

5. How would changing your expectations to God's expectations—obedience—improve your relationship with Christ?

74

God's Ways Bring Fulfillment

> I meditate on your precepts
> and consider your ways.
> I delight in your decrees;
> I will not neglect your word.

Psalm 119:15–16

Growing up, I dreamed of finding a spouse, having children, and nurturing my family," a sixty-six-year-old woman named Audrey told me. "It went beyond the stigma that was attached to singleness in the 1950s, although I certainly wanted to avoid the stigma. But I just couldn't imagine my future without a spouse and children."

While attending a Christian college, she met a man with whom she fell in love, and they got married. She was convinced that her dream had come true. She couldn't have been more wrong. Her husband turned out to be bisexual, and her dream came crashing down when they divorced.

For many years after that, she battled with her old expectations of finding someone to love her. I recently asked her what she did to overcome those expectations. "I realized I lacked the spiritual knowledge necessary to live a normal life," she said. "I prayed for years, 'Lord, teach me what you want me to know,' and he did just that."

She started reading Christian books and studying her Bible. As her knowledge grew, she started discipling other people. That's when she realized God was calling her to help people recognize who they are in Christ. As she helped people, she recognized a new attitude developing about her expectations of finding a spouse—they were disappearing.

She was aligning her expectations with God's by delighting herself in God's decrees and seeking to help others. "In the past, I would meet someone I thought might be a suitable mate, and I would begin to obsess, to plan, to pray for opportunities to be with him," she said.

She now feels free to pursue a relationship if God opens that door, but her expectations no longer govern her life. As a result, she is helping people grow in their faith and enjoying each day that God gives her.

DIGGING DEEPER INTO PSALM 119:15–16

1. How does the way Audrey dealt with her expectations of finding a spouse compare or contrast with the way you deal with your own expectations?

2. Do you find God's decrees a delight or a drudgery? Explain.

3. How much time do you spend each week meditating on God's precepts and considering his ways?

4. Do you spend more time thinking about his ways than you do thinking about your expectations of finding a spouse? Explain.

5. What could you do that would help you to focus your energy on helping others?

75

Good Expectations

Follow my example, as I follow the example of Christ.

1 Corinthians 11:1

Not all expectations are negative. Some spur us on to live the life God has called us to. The above verse is an example of this. At the end of 1 Corinthians 10, the apostle Paul instructed believers in Corinth to be less concerned about such things as eating meat that had been sacrificed to idols than they were about causing someone to stumble in their faith journey.

Then he said, "For I am not seeking my own good but the good of many, so that they may be saved" (1 Cor. 10:33). Paul set the example and expected the Corinthian church, and every other believer, to follow. We are to reach out to unbelievers, even when their lifestyle clashes with ours.

Paul's expectation for us comes from his position of authority over us. Similarly, when our parents expect us to take over the family business, or take a job in a certain field, or graduate from college, or anything else, their expectations come from people who have a position of authority in our lives. That position of authority changes when we become adults, but no matter what our stage of life, we need to consider our parents' expectations, because God may be trying to tell us something.

However, just because one or both of our parents tell us to "follow their example" doesn't mean we should automatically do so. If after spending time in prayer and seeking godly counsel we determine that these expectations are not what God intends for our lives, we can reject them as gently and lovingly as possible. But don't be too quick to discount their advice, because God can use them to speak to us.

Legitimate expectations, like Paul's in the verse above, raise the level of our performance bar to places we might not otherwise attempt. While those in authority over us might sometimes have skewed intentions with their expectations for us, many of their intentions flow from love.

DIGGING DEEPER INTO 1 CORINTHIANS 11:1

1. What are your thoughts about the apostle Paul's expectations for you in this verse?

2. How willing are you to listen to your parents when they share their expectations of you?

3. How has God used their expectations in the past to spur you on to do something he wanted you to do?

4. What process do you normally go through after hearing their expectations (e.g., automatic dismissal, prayer, discussion)?

5. How will this verse change the way you react in the future to your parents' expectations?

76

My Expectation Is from Him

> My soul, wait silently for God alone,
> For my expectation is from Him.
>
> Psalm 62:5 NKJV

Nancy, twenty-nine years old, is content in her single-ness. Like all of us, she sometimes struggles with loneliness, but she believes that God is in control of her marital status. She just wishes that her family and friends believed the same thing.

"People often assume I'm not married because I'm not ready, somehow not mature enough, as though married people are inherently on a higher plane of self-actualization than single people," she explained. Like Nancy, we all face expectations from friends or loved ones about our single-ness. The pressure can be overwhelming.

When facing such pressure, Nancy often thinks about her favorite joke: "I used to get annoyed with all the grand-mother types coming up to me at weddings and saying, 'You're next!' They stopped doing that after I began doing the same thing to them at funerals."

In all seriousness, waiting silently for God and drawing our expectations from him is the only way to keep other people's expectations in perspective. God knows the future. He knows his plans for us. Those who try to impose their expectations on us do not know what will happen one min-ute from now, and they certainly do not know the perfect plans God has for us in the future.

Nancy understands this well. "I believe I'm not in a re-lationship right now because God has a plan that I am seeking to understand and carry out. How could a plan from God for one person's life be any less perfect or valid than his plan for another person's life?"

How indeed? When our expectation comes from God, as the psalm states, that is the way we will feel.

1. Who in your life is trying to get you to live up to their expectations?

2. How have you responded to them?

3. Explain how you felt the last time you took a loved one's negative words to heart. Do you believe God wants you to feel this way?

4. How are you seeking God's plan for your life right now? Are you waiting silently for him alone?

5. How will you respond the next time a loved one tries to impose his or her expectations on you?

77

Eating with Unwashed Hands

> Then the Pharisees and scribes asked Him, "Why do
> Your disciples not walk according to the tradition of the
> elders, but eat bread with unwashed hands?"
>
> Mark 7:5 NKJV

The Pharisees had a problem with the followers of Jesus. His disciples didn't wash their hands "in a special way" (Mark 7:3 NKJV) before eating according to the Pharisees' tradition. In the Pharisees' minds, the followers of Jesus were unclean because they didn't follow this tradition. They had elevated their traditions above the law of God with the intention of achieving holiness. The law of God doesn't instruct everyone to be cleansed before eating—only the priests who performed a sacrifice (Exod. 30:17–21).

Jesus refused to allow the Pharisees' expectations to dictate the actions of his followers, so he used the Old Testament to instruct them in this. In Mark 7:6–7, Jesus used similar words to those of the prophet Isaiah (29:13): "This people honors Me with their lips, but their heart is far from Me. And in vain they worship Me, teaching as doctrines the commandments of men" (NKJV).

Jesus used strong words to answer the Pharisees' expectations. He didn't hint that they had hurt his feelings like we sometimes do when someone tries to get us to live up to his or her expectations. And he didn't feel pressured to go along with them like we sometimes do. He simply told them that their traditions had nothing to do with God's way of preparing for a meal; therefore he wouldn't submit to those traditions. Jesus wasn't against good hygiene; he was against the traditions of men being seen as more important than the law of God.

The way Jesus handled himself is a great example for us when someone tries to get us to live up to his or her expectations for us. What would happen if we handled those people in the same fashion that Jesus did? Perhaps a simple statement about not being willing to live up to somebody else's expectations for us would go a long way toward them backing off. It might make us uncomfortable for a moment or two, but isn't a moment of discomfort worth the payoff?

DIGGING DEEPER INTO MARK 7:5

1. How does the person or people who have certain expectations of you consider you "unclean" or missing the mark?

2. How does the way you've responded to this person compare or contrast to the way Jesus handled the Pharisees?

3. How successful has your way been to deter the person from harping on you?

4. Do you still feel pressure from this person, or have you been able to rest in knowing that you are in God's will for this period of time in your life?

5. How willing are you to be as firm as necessary with this person, knowing that it may cause a moment of discomfort?

78

Parental Pressure

> The LORD had said to Abram, "Leave your country, your people and your father's household and go to the land I will show you."
>
> Genesis 12:1

We move more frequently than people used to. Extended family now often live on the other side of the country instead of the other side of the block. We move for college, jobs, love, and many other reasons. No matter what the reason, however, parents are rarely crazy about the idea. Unless, of course, we've overstayed our welcome in their homes.

Seriously though, the pressure we can feel from our parents' expectations to stay in their same city or region of the country can be burdensome. We wonder whether an impending move would somehow violate the fifth commandment to honor our father and mother. We fear hearing "I told you so" from them if the move doesn't work out as planned. Finally, we just don't like to disappoint them.

It appears that Abram's father, Terah, intended to take his family to Canaan, but they settled in Haran (Gen. 11:31). God did not intend for Abram to travel to Canaan with his father, as the verse above mentions. At the age of seventy-five (12:4), Abram set out from Haran for Canaan, leaving his father in Haran, where Terah eventually died (11:32) many years later.

We aren't told how Terah felt about Abram leaving his household. We do know that God told Abram to leave his father's household because God had other plans for Abram. Perhaps he thought he could bring his father with him to

Canaan and still accomplish what God wanted him to do, but he left after realizing he was wrong.

Though we aren't told whether Abram felt pressure to stay with his father, we do know that he placed a higher priority on God's will than his father's will—even though he apparently compromised at first. If he did feel pressure, then he decided to do the right thing in spite of it. If he didn't, his willingness to obey God is still a good example for us to follow the next time we consider a move.

DIGGING DEEPER INTO GENESIS 12:1

1. When you contemplate a move, how much weight do you give your parents' expectations for you to stay in the area you live in?

2. Describe your mental struggle with pleasing your parents versus doing what you think God wants you to do.

3. How has the fifth commandment come into play as you've thought about moving to a different area of the country?

4. How has your fear of hearing "I told you so" affected your decision to go or stay?

5. If you believed God was telling you to go, would you go—regardless of your thoughts or fears?

79

Dealing with Stumbling Blocks

> Jesus turned and said to Peter, "Get behind me, Satan! You are a stumbling block to me; you do not have in mind the things of God, but the things of men."
>
> Matthew 16:23

Peter loved Jesus. Understandably, he had a hard time hearing Jesus talk about traveling to Jerusalem in order to die. In fact, he was unwilling to accept it. Here he stood with the long-awaited Messiah who was about to usher in God's kingdom, and Jesus was talking about dying.

How could the Messiah usher in the kingdom of God if he was going to die? Peter's expectations for the Messiah were the same as those of many other believers at that time: Jesus would lead the people of God in a conquest of Rome and set up his kingdom here on earth. But Jesus didn't come in the flesh to conquer Rome. He came to conquer sin and death. He didn't need to come in the flesh to conquer kings. He already was and is the King of Kings.

Peter's expectations for the Messiah led him to rebuke Jesus after he discovered that Jesus was going to die. "Never, Lord!" he said. "This shall never happen to you!" Jesus loved Peter, but he recognized that Satan was at work in him, so he put an end to Peter's objection by telling him that he had his mind on the things of men instead of God.

Expectations can lead to wrong conclusions. People can't possibly know for sure what God has in store for us, so consequently they can become a stumbling block to us—much as Peter was to Jesus in the verse above.

That doesn't mean we should reject all counsel or rebukes. But when we determine that the counsel or rebuke is "of men" and not God, we must see these people as stumbling blocks. Like Jesus, we must be up front with them and be concerned about only the things of God.

1. Have you ever considered the people in your life who have certain expectations for you as stumbling blocks?

2. Jesus defined a stumbling block as someone who did not have in mind the things of God but of man. How does knowing this help you deal with people who have expectations?

3. What have you told your stumbling blocks when they have rebuked you in the past?

4. How does your answer compare or contrast to Jesus's answer?

5. If you were to handle stumbling blocks sternly, how do you think it would stop friends or relatives from continually putting pressure on you?

80

A Friend on a Mission

> I will lead the blind by ways they have not known,
> along unfamiliar paths I will guide them;
> I will turn the darkness into light before them
> and make the rough places smooth.
> These are the things I will do;
> I will not forsake them.
>
> Isaiah 42:16

When Wayne moved from Southern California to Seattle last year, he wanted to keep in touch with his friends, and he found email a great way to do it. One of his friends is a woman he met in college. She is now married and has two children. She seems to be on a mission to make sure that Wayne also gets married. His other friends ask him how he likes Seattle, how his new job is going, and whether he's found a good church to attend. His married female friend doesn't ask those questions.

"The first question she asks me is, 'So, have you found anyone you're interested in yet?'" Wayne said. Her expectations are frustrating for him. After he tells her that he hasn't been looking, she backs off temporarily, "but it sure does kill the conversation when that's the only thing she wants to know about my life, as opposed to the things I'm actually doing," Wayne said.

As frustrated as Wayne gets about her expectations, he realizes that the only expectations that matter are those placed on him by God. In the verse above, God promises to lead and guide us along "unfamiliar paths." He's the only one who knows our future, so when we are feeling pressure from someone in our lives to marry, we can cling to God and his plans.

Wayne understands this well. "It's enough for me to keep in mind that no matter what other people expect of me, God is the only one I really need to answer to. If I'm truly following God's will (and I know I often struggle with that), then if other people are disappointed with the way I live my life, it's their own fault for having misguided expectations," he said.

DIGGING DEEPER INTO ISAIAH 42:16

1. Do you have any married friends, as Wayne does, who seem to be more concerned with your marital status than anything else in your life? List them here.

2. How have you handled their constant questions about your marital status?

3. Do you feel pressured by the questions they ask, or can you say that you are resting in God's plan for the future? Explain.

4. How would your friends react if you told them that you are trusting God with your future and that you will continue seeking his will?

5. How has this devotion prepared you for pressures to conform to someone's expectations in the future?

Part 9

Embracing Life

L uci Swindoll is a single with a vibrant life. She owns
her own art studio. She gardens. She writes. She speaks
to women and singles all over the country. And if you have
ever heard her speak, you've heard her enthusiasm for life,
which leaves no doubt that she embraces the life God has
given her.

She's not the only single who is embracing life. You'll
meet several singles in this section whom you have probably
never heard of before. They are embracing the life God has
given them. And if you have heard of them, it's because God
is using them in ways they never imagined. By embracing
life, these and so many other singles like them are making
a difference for the kingdom of God.

Are you at that stage in your life where you can honestly say that you embrace the life God has given you as a
single person? God has given each of us ministry opportunities—to help people in need, to serve in missions, to
open our homes for some good, old-fashioned hospitality,
and the list goes on and on.

Beyond the opportunities to embrace life through service,
we have the chance to embrace life by purchasing a home,

planning for retirement, starting a college savings plan for our nephew or niece, taking dance lessons, writing a novel, playing guitar, or painting a work of art.

In some cases, the only chance we will ever have to do some of these things is right now. So why wait? God gives all of us seasons in life, and once he determines that any particular season is finished, we never get a chance to relive it. Think about what you could be missing right now.

For the next ten days, we will study what the Bible says about embracing the life God has given you. I pray that this section will change the way you live your life this very day. Putting it together for you has changed the way I'm living. These singles have challenged and inspired me to embrace life.

81

Do What Your Hand Finds to Do

> Whatever your hand finds to do, do it with all your might,
> for in the grave, where you are going, there is neither
> working nor planning nor knowledge nor wisdom.
>
> Ecclesiastes 9:10

Several years ago, I met a thirtysomething single Christian writer named Christin. She has written thirty-five books and has her own national radio program. She also has an extended family whom she loves and is involved with. She lives a full life.

"I don't let my marital status define who I am," she said. "No matter how demanding my job is or how many other obligations I have, being single gives me a lot of freedom and flexibility. I can counsel a friend on the phone for three hours without interruption. I can work through the night to meet a deadline. The truth is that the only way I could possibly do all the things I do now is because I'm single."

That doesn't change the fact that Christin still wants to be married; it simply changes her attitude about this season in her life. "Some days I'm overwhelmed by the desire to have someone to share my life with—no matter what I'd have to give up for it," she says, "times when I'm really weary of carrying all the responsibilities of life on my own. I'd like someone else to balance the checkbook or take out the garbage or squash the spiders. But when I get past that, I recognize that being single enables me to be extremely productive during this particular season of my life." Christin lives the principle of doing whatever her hand finds to do with all her might.

"The key is to remember that seasons change," she says. "The way my life is now is not how it will be forever. Somehow, you've got to keep that in perspective and learn to appreciate where you are."

DIGGING DEEPER INTO ECCLESIASTES 9:10

1. God probably hasn't called you to write thirty-five books, but he has called you to do something right now that only you can do. What is it?

2. Are you doing it "with all your might"? Explain.

3. What better defines you—your status as a single person or your status as a believer in Jesus Christ? Explain.

4. List all of the things you are able to do right now that you would not be able to do if you were married.

5. How are you showing God that you appreciate the time he has given you to do what he has called you to do?

82

Embracing Time Alone

> I would like you to be free from concern. An unmarried man is concerned about the Lord's affairs—how he can please the Lord.
>
> 1 Corinthians 7:32

Recently, I traveled almost two hundred miles alone to participate in the Nebraska state bowling tournament. I popped an R. C. Sproul sermon into my CD player. In his message from Colossians 2–3, he spoke about "setting our minds on things above."

Several hours after listening to the sermon, I was still thinking about his message and how I could apply it to my life. I realized that if I had been traveling with someone else, my chances of concentrating exclusively on the message would not have been high. And even if I had, I would not have had all the time I did to think about the message afterward.

Traveling by myself, I was "free from concern," as 1 Corinthians 7:32 says, to focus on the things of God. Traveling with someone else might have led to a battle over the contents of the CD player.

For these reasons, I'm beginning to enjoy traveling by myself. I wouldn't always want to do it, but it is one of the few times in my life beyond my daily devotional time that I am not "doing" something. I haven't always used my travel time as productively as I did on this particular trip, but experiencing the benefits of "the Lord's affairs" has motivated me to spend my travel time more wisely in the future.

I felt closer to God that particular morning than I had in quite awhile. As I walked into the bowling center later that day, I couldn't shake the great feeling that it was a good day to be single.

DIGGING DEEPER INTO 1 CORINTHIANS 7:32

1. Before this devotion, what was your normal reaction to this verse when you read it?

2. Do you enjoy traveling by yourself? Why or why not?

3. How can you incorporate 1 Corinthians 7:32 into your future travels?

4. How can your singleness be an opportunity to draw closer to God?

5. Has looking deeper into this verse helped change your perspective about this verse?

83

Joy in Service

> You, my brothers, were called to be free. But do not use
> your freedom to indulge the sinful nature; rather, serve
> one another in love.
>
> Galatians 5:13

When LeAnne's husband abandoned her and their daughter, she clung to God as she never had before. "Being so close to him helped me reach a place of contentment so much more quickly than I could have done on my own," said LeAnne.

That place of contentment has shaped her new life. "I'm enjoying discovering who I am at this point in my life," she said. "Even though I never planned to be single again, my life is full—with raising my daughter, pursuing new interests, and helping lead a small group. I'm purposefully living my life right now—rather than living in limbo until another husband comes along. I don't want to waste my life waiting for someone who may never come along anyway."

The verse above indicates that we have a choice to make regarding our liberty. We can use it to indulge our sinful nature, or we can use it to serve others. LeAnne is using her freedom to serve at her church by leading a small group for single mothers.

I asked her what she would say to singles who feel called to serve in church or elsewhere but resist because they want to be married before they begin serving. She didn't hesitate to offer encouragement: "Don't wait," she said. "Please don't wait! As a single, you are free to pursue the ministry opportunities that most tug at your heart. It's through serving and loving the Lord and his people with the gifts and skill set he has given you that you will find fulfillment—if you allow yourself to. If you wait until you're married, you will have missed out, possibly, on some incredible opportunities to make an impact for the kingdom of God and to grow as a person."

DIGGING DEEPER INTO GALATIANS 5:13

1. How content are you with your life right now?

2. Do you feel you have a purpose, or are you drifting?

3. According to Galatians 5:13, what are we as Christians called to do with our lives?

4. How are you using your freedom by serving singles or other people in your church?

5. What is the correlation between the time you have or have not spent in service to others to the amount of fulfillment you currently feel?

84

Celebrating Valentine's Day as a Single

> My command is this: Love each other as I have loved you.
>
> John 15:12

When you think about what Jesus said to his disciples in the above verse, it seems intimidating doesn't it? You and I are to love each other the way Jesus loved us. It is hard to imagine how that is possible, but just because we cannot imagine it doesn't mean we are free to ignore his command.

Some singles are experiencing the joy that comes from loving other believers for who they are, not as potential spouses. They are investing their lives in other believers by breaking bread with them, listening to their concerns, serving them, and enjoying their fellowship.

One of those singles is a twenty-five-year-old woman named Irene. Recently she accepted the invitation of her friend Sarah to celebrate Valentine's Day on a picnic with some of Sarah's friends. On a day when it is far too easy for singles to feel sorry for themselves, Irene and Sarah were proactive.

"We spread a mat on the grass," Irene said. "Slipped a Josh Groban CD into the player, drank sparkling grape juice, ate pizza and munched potato chips, and talked about anything and everything, laughing a lot. It was possibly the most enjoyable Valentine's Day I've had in all my twenty-five years. I skipped a family dinner for it and have no regrets."[7]

What a great way to spend Valentine's Day!

Changes in lifestyles happen one day at a time and one step of obedience at a time. When I think about what Jesus commanded me to do in the verse above, too often I think about his command in the context of the rest of my life, and it just does not seem possible. I am just as susceptible to giving in to my selfish needs as anybody else. But when I think about following his command today, I'm challenged to obey. Are you?

DIGGING DEEPER INTO JOHN 15:12

1. What is the first thing that comes to mind when you think about the command Jesus gave us in John 15:12?

2. Do you spend more time seeking love from people you consider to be a potential spouse than you do from other believers? Explain.

3. How is Irene and Sarah's Valentine's Day celebration similar or different from the way you normally spend that holiday?

4. When you think about Jesus's command, do you consider it in the context of your entire life or just today?

5. How has this devotion challenged you to obey his command?

85

Planning Financially for the Future

> If anyone does not provide for his relatives, and especially for his immediate family, he has denied the faith and is worse than an unbeliever.
>
> 1 Timothy 5:8

As we contemplate our future, one thing we need to examine is money—as in whether we are saving enough of it to provide for ourselves when we get older. Linda Hardin, general coordinator of single adult ministries and women's ministries for the Church of the Nazarene denomination, reminds us that "God requires us to be good stewards of the finances we have. I believe that includes preparing for the future."

She knows that some Christian singles are not planning financially for the future because they barely make enough money to cover their current expenses. But as a single herself, she has discovered that a little sacrifice right now pays great dividends in the future. "I've found that I learn to live on whatever amount of money is available. It's amazing the little things I can do to cut expenses—adjust the heat or air-conditioning, take my lunch to work frequently, prepare dinner at home rather than eating out, and shop sales."

By cutting expenses for the past several years, Hardin has been able to put money into the retirement plan offered by the denomination she works for. She has also purchased a life insurance policy, an IRA, and even put a little into savings.

First Timothy 5:8 instructs men to provide financially for their families. The apostle Paul does not consider this a worldly endeavor in the least. In fact, he said if a man does not do it, he has denied the faith. Single believers are the heads of their own households and therefore responsible for providing for themselves.

If you do not know where to start, Hardin offers this advice: "Talk with someone who can provide information to make informed decisions to plan for the future. Talk to your pastor and find out if he knows anybody who can help you. Check with your human resources department to see if they offer free financial advice. Talk to a banker. Or spend a little time researching safe investments. Years from now, you'll be glad you did."

DIGGING DEEPER INTO 1 TIMOTHY 5:8

1. What have you done to prepare for your future financially?

2. How could you be doing more?

3. How does this Scripture motivate you to do more?

4. Name three things in your current lifestyle you could cut back on so you could invest more money into a plan to provide for your future.

5. List at least two people from whom you can seek financial planning advice and commit to meeting with them in the near future.

86

Gathering for the Harvest

> Go to the ant, you sluggard;
>   consider its ways and be wise!
> It has no commander,
>   no overseer or ruler,
> yet it stores its provisions in summer
>   and gathers its food at harvest.
>
> Proverbs 6:6–8

J oy is an experienced home buyer. "I purchased a condo in the late eighties, when I was in my late twenties," she said. "I had rented a few apartments before, but I knew it wasn't a wise use of money because there is no return on it. I wasn't happy with the last rental neighborhood I lived in or the constant turnover of residents. I knew if I saved enough money for a substantial down payment, my mortgage would not be that much more than rent. I also wanted a place to call my own. I felt it was a good investment, and it just made good sense."

When the opportunity came along to purchase a home that needed quite a bit of work, Joy decided to buy it. Her condo was easier to maintain because she had to pay only a set maintenance fee, but she didn't have the freedom that comes with owning a house because her condo had strict association bylaws she had to follow. With that freedom, however, she had to maintain the house herself—something she has struggled to do. But she thinks it has been worth it.

"I like living in the country. It's quiet and peaceful here, and in the five years I've lived here, the value of my home has increased by approximately $45,000. And it's projected to increase even more," she said.

She considers the increase in value vitally important for her future. "It's the only investment I have at this time, and it's encouraging to know that if I stay here until I retire, I should be able to sell it and make enough profit to live comfortably in a less expensive county or state if necessary."

Joy is a living example of the passage above from Proverbs. She is storing up provisions while it is summer because she knows fall is coming. She has done what she can to ensure that she will be able to gather a harvest when she is older. Consequently she will be free to devote time to whatever the Lord may have for her in later years.

DIGGING DEEPER INTO PROVERBS 6:6–8

1. Describe your thoughts about buying a house.

2. What role has your marital status played in your previous housing decision making?

3. If you are not currently a homeowner, how might your purchase of a home right now provide financially for your harvest years?

4. What is the possibility that you have avoided purchasing a home because you fear that it would solidify your feeling that you are going to remain single?

5. Name three freedoms that you would have if you purchased a home that you don't currently have in your present living condition.

87

Your Life Has Already Begun

> I am not saying this because I am in need, for I have
> learned to be content whatever the circumstances.
>
> Philippians 4:11

I don't dwell on my singleness or allow people to make me feel that something is wrong with me for not being married," says Charlesetta, a forty-three-year-old single woman who has learned how to embrace life.

Her life includes a job with the federal government and service in her church. She is currently involved in the music ministry in her church, and in the past she has led singles and young adult ministries. She also believes that maintaining close friendships with other believers (single and married) helps her to live a full life.

When I asked her what Scripture verse has best helped her live this way, she pointed to the verse above. Like Paul, Charlesetta has learned to be content. Paul shared what he called the "secret" to contentment a few verses later. "I can do everything through him who gives me strength" (Phil. 4:13).

God gave Paul a mission and empowered him to take the gospel throughout Asia Minor. Paul knew he couldn't do anything apart from Christ—especially something as monumental as taking the gospel to the Gentile world. He also knew that God intended for him to be single in order to accomplish his will.

For now, God intends for you and me to be single in order to accomplish his will—to do that one thing that comes to your mind and to mine each time we ponder his will. Your task may be large in scope, like Paul's, or it may be smaller. Whatever it is, embrace it as your calling.

"Since you don't know God's timetable, focus on your present," Charlesetta says. "Don't think that life will begin when you marry. Your life has already begun. Live it to the fullest!"

DIGGING DEEPER INTO PHILIPPIANS 4:11

1. How do you put your life on hold?

2. How content do you feel right now?

3. Paul's secret to contentment was to live in Christ's strength. How well are you doing that? How can you do it better?

4. What one thing pops into your mind immediately when you think about God's will for your life and what you know he has called you to do?

5. If you're not currently doing it, when will you start?

88

Postcard Hospitality

> Share with God's people who are in need. Practice
> hospitality.
>
> Romans 12:13

If you have ever walked into a new church and sat down
in a Sunday school class or small group meeting, you
know how intimidating that can be. Will this new group of
people accept you? Will you find good friends there? Will
you finally feel at home in a church? Or will the environment feel colder than two strangers standing next to each
other in an elevator but refusing to make eye contact?

If you had a woman in your class like Vikki, your concerns
would quickly fade. Vikki goes to a singles Sunday school
class in a church I used to attend. Occasionally I visited the
class she was in, and without fail, I later received a postcard
from her telling me how welcome I was in the class and
that I was welcome to return any time.

The motivation behind her hospitality is simple. Vikki
says that she puts herself in the new person's position and
treats that person the way she would like to be treated—the
Golden Rule put into practice. She sends out postcards to
every new person who visits her class, offering them words
of encouragement with an invitation to come back.

She's also been known to drop postcards in the mail
to classmates she hasn't seen for a while. In an age when
it is far too easy to walk into a new church, attend a class
and a worship service, and then walk out without anybody
ever acknowledging you, people like Vikki are rare. So rare
that I've never met anybody else who keeps up with classmates—both new and old—like she does.

Practicing hospitality, as the verse above tells all of us to do, is a natural part of Vikki's life. Not because she's a supersaint but because she is a saint who seeks to serve her Savior well.

1. When was the last time you walked into a new church and left without anybody showing you he or she genuinely cared that you were there?

2. Conversely, when was the last time you walked into a new church and met someone like Vikki who made you feel welcome?

3. Which scenario best describes the atmosphere of your current Sunday school class or small group?

4. How do you currently practice hospitality?

5. How could practicing hospitality more often lead to a more fulfilling life?

89

The Freedom to Go

> I have come that they may have life, and have it to the full.
>
> John 10:10

Melanie never dreamed that she would go on seven mission trips to Russia. But as a thirty-one-year-old single, she believes, "There is a freedom that exists when you do not have another person to consider. It is not just a tangible freedom, such as not having to coordinate schedules; it is also a freedom of the heart to be free to fully love and be fully there without a desire or need to return home to a spouse."

Melanie is living the life Jesus promised in the verse above. "I am here to serve Jesus and have no right to say what form that will take. It simply doesn't matter if I want to have kids, have a spouse, live in the suburbs, or whatever," she says. "I may never have a spouse or a child, own a home, or make a lot of money, but I have life and have it to the full."

She entered into this phase of her life by simply being open to God's leading. "I read in my bulletin one Sunday back in the summer of 1999 about a team going to Kursk, Russia, and God spoke to my heart that I was to go. Since then I have absolutely fallen in love with the people of Russia and their hunger for hope and life that is found in Christ alone."

Listen to the attitude she has about the sacrifices she has made in order to spend time with the people she loves from Russia: "I love seeing people come alive and hearts transformed by the healing message of Jesus Christ. It is worth every dollar, every unpaid day off work, and any other sacrifice that I have been called to make."

By serving Jesus where he has called her to go, she finds joy in sacrifice. She finds life in the death of her desires. She finds abundance in her lack. At a relatively young age, she has found what many people, including Christians, never do.

DIGGING DEEPER INTO JOHN 10:10

1. Have you ever seen your singleness the way Melanie does in the first paragraph of this devotion? Why or why not?

2. How are you currently experiencing the full life Jesus promised in John 10:10?

3. When you think about living a full life, what does it look like?

4. If you read a church bulletin, a book, or anything else and felt led by God to service, how willing would you be to obey him?

5. Melanie sees great value in sacrifice in regard to finding a full life. How does your attitude toward sacrifice compare or contrast with hers?

90

I Like Being Single

The LORD will watch over your coming and going
both now and forevermore.

Psalm 121:8

Torry Martin travels all across the United States performing as a Christian comedian at various conferences, cruises, and retreats. He also writes novels, humor columns, and episodes of *Adventures in Odyssey* for Focus on the Family. Listen to his "embracing life" attitude: "There is no doubt in my mind that the reason I'm single right now is because God wanted me to be available for ministry," he told me. "I actually feel called to remain single, and I wouldn't have it any other way."

In addition, he sees his ministry in much broader terms than just his comedy and writing. "I like being single and being available to do whatever God wants me to do," he said. "Whether that's just traveling to see my friends, or going on a mission trip at a moment's notice, or just spending time interceding for others." He goes on to say, "My greatest ministry is having the time to be a good friend to the people in my life who are important."

Torry points to the verse above as motivation for him to embrace life right now. "Knowing that God's got his eye on me *forever*, whether I remain single or marry, brings me great comfort and encourages me to embrace whatever comes my way."

He also has some great advice for singles. "I don't think God is really waiting for people to get married before he can use them to their full potential. Look at the apostle Paul. He wasn't married, and God used him all over the place.

And what about Mother Teresa? Do you think anyone ever told her that she wasn't living a fulfilled life just because she wasn't married? Or what about the professor on *Gilligan's Island*? He wasn't married, and that guy was a genius!"

Torry is obviously not afraid to use his comedic talent to make a spiritual point. Something he does quite well.

DIGGING DEEPER INTO PSALM 121:8

1. List the ministries that God has given to you—including those you can use to support and encourage your friends and family.

2. Do you believe that you would be able to put as much time, effort, and prayer into all of your ministries if you were married right now? Explain.

3. Have you ever thanked God for giving these ministries to you? If not, take the time to do so now.

4. Does Psalm 121:8 comfort you and encourage you to embrace life right now the way it does Torry?

5. Do you believe that God is waiting for you to be married before he will use you to your full potential? Explain.

Notes

1. Jo Kadlecek, *Feast of Life* (Grand Rapids: Baker, 1999), 111.

2. Harold Ivan Smith, *Movers & Shapers: Singles Who Changed Their World* (Old Tappan, NJ: Revell, 1988), 185.

3. Gina Kim, "Wedding-day kiss will be couple's first," *Seattle Times,* August 9, 2003, http://archives.seattletime.nwsource.com/cgi-bin/texis.cgi/web/vortex/display?slug+kiss09&date=20030809

4. Matthew Henry, *Complete Commentary on the Whole Bible,* http://bible.crosswalk.com/Commentaries/MatthewHenryComplete/mhc-com.cgi?book=ps&chapter=037.

5. Ibid.

6. "Some Christian Guy," blog, November 3, 2003, http://somechristianguy.com/archives/2003_11.html

7. "As I Wait," February 16, 2004, http://ireneq.com/guardheart/archives/000953.html. Used by permission.

Lee Warren is a freelance writer from Omaha, Nebraska. He is the former *Christianity Today* online singles columnist, and he has written more than a hundred articles for publications such as *Discipleship Journal, Decision, Sports Spectrum, Sharing the VICTORY, Light & Life, War Cry*, and many others. If you are interested in reading more of Lee's material for singles, please visit www.singleservings.net.